FOR US THE LIVING

FOR US THE LIVING

THE CIVIL WAR
IN PAINTINGS AND
EYEWITNESS ACCOUNTS

MORT KÜNSTLER

Text by James I. Robertson Jr.

Foreword by Harold Holzer

STERLING

New York / London
www.sterlingpublishing.com

STERLING and the distinctive Sterling logo are registered trademarks of
Sterling Publishing Co., Inc.

Library of Congress Cataloging-in-Publication Data

Künstler, Mort.
  For us the living : the Civil War in paintings and eyewitness accounts / Mort Künstler ;
text by James I. Robertson Jr. ; foreword by Harold Holzer.
     p. cm.
  Includes bibliographical references and index.
  ISBN 978–1–4027–7034–0
  1. United States—History—Civil War, 1861–1865—Pictorial works. 2. United States—
History—Civil War, 1861–1865—Art and the war. 3. United States—History—Civil War,
1861–1865—Personal narratives. I. Robertson, James I. II. Title.
  E468.7.K843 2010
  973.7—dc22
                              2010012837

10 9 8 7 6 5 4 3 2 1

Published by Sterling Publishing Co., Inc.
387 Park Avenue South, New York, NY 10016

Distributed in Canada by Sterling Publishing
c/o Canadian Manda Group, 165 Dufferin Street
Toronto, Ontario, Canada M6K 3H6
Distributed in the United Kingdom by GMC Distribution Services
Castle Place, 166 High Street, Lewes, East Sussex, England BN7 1XU
Distributed in Australia by Capricorn Link (Australia) Pty. Ltd.
P.O. Box 704, Windsor, NSW 2756, Australia

A Creative Media Applications production
Interior design and production: Fabia Wargin
Copy-editing: Laurie Lieb

Sterling ISBN 978–1–4027–7034–0

For information about custom editions, special sales, premium and
corporate purchases, please contact Sterling Special Sales
Department at 800–805–5489 or specialsales@sterlingpublishing.com.

FRONTISPIECE: Detail, *Salute of Honor,* Appomattox, April 12, 1865

To my family

— M Künstler

FOUR SCORE AND SEVEN YEARS AGO OUR FATHERS BROUGHT forth on this continent, a new nation, conceived in Liberty, and dedicated to the proposition that all men are created equal.

Now we are engaged in a great civil war, testing whether that nation, or any nation so conceived and so dedicated, can long endure. We are met on a great battlefield of that war. We have come to dedicate a portion of that field, as a final resting place for those who here gave their lives that that nation might live. It is altogether fitting and proper that we should do this.

But, in a larger sense, we can not dedicate—we can not consecrate—we can not hallow—this ground. The brave men, living and dead, who struggled here, have consecrated it, far above our poor power to add or detract. The world will little note, nor long remember what we say here, but it can never forget what they did here. It is FOR US THE LIVING, rather, to be dedicated here to the unfinished work which they who fought here have thus far so nobly advanced. It is rather for us to be here dedicated to the great task remaining before us—that from these honored dead we take increased devotion to that cause for which they gave the last full measure of devotion—that we here highly resolve that these dead shall not have died in vain— that this nation, under God, shall have a new birth of freedom—and that government of the people, by the people, for the people, shall not perish from the earth.

PRESIDENT ABRAHAM LINCOLN
Gettysburg, Pennsylvania · November 19, 1863

ABRAHAM LINCOLN, *Gettysburg Address Portrait*

CONTENTS

FOREWORD

"THE WAR ITSELF HAS NOT inspired many works" of art, *Harper's Weekly* observed disdainfully in the spring of 1862, after the country had endured some thirteen months of grueling—and, one would have thought, picturesque—military strife. Two years of memorable battle and sacrifice later, yet another publication, the *Round Table,* observed little improvement in the state of artistic attention, lamenting, "One of the most remarkable circumstances connected with the existing war is the very remote and trifling influence which it seems to have exerted upon American Art."

Perhaps these observers were not looking in the right places. Illustrated newsweeklies like *Harper's,* for example, had by then themselves opened a revealing window onto the war with their seemingly endless series of front-line woodcuts. In the bargain they served as a valuable training ground for immortal artists of the near future like Winslow Homer and Thomas Nast.

Not that formal works of art were being neglected, for, from the beginning, serious painters did produce them, albeit in the shadows. In the South, for example, accomplished landscape artist William D. Washington had already turned his keen eye and deft brush to the Union-Confederate struggle for the picturesque terrain of the Virginia mountains. Among Northern artists, Sanford Robinson Gifford had traveled productively with New York's 7th Regiment, undertaking a series of magnificent pastoral canvases of Union troops encamped in the bluffs above Arlington. Marine artist Xanthus Smith was on board a Federal vessel of war making sketches he would soon adapt into robust canvases. And Conrad Wise Chapman, under the supervision of Confederate general P. G. T. Beauregard, was busily painting a magnificent series of oils on board showing the defenses in Charleston Harbor.

Thus, almost from the opening guns, professional artists, soldier-artists, prisoner-artists, and artist correspondents all labored diligently and creatively to take the measure of both individual incidents, and the broader meaning, of the all-engrossing conflict. In Washington, Abraham Lincoln posed for an official portrait as early as 1863. In Richmond, Jefferson Davis did likewise. And by 1864, artists were traveling with both Ulysses S. Grant and Robert E. Lee, determined to immortalize them on campaign.

Then why did so few "expert" observers fail to understand the contributions that artists indeed made, almost from the outset of the fighting, to our understanding of the Civil War and the valor and sacrifice of both military and civilian leaders, common soldiers, and home-front eyewitnesses?

To understand this anomaly of reputation requires an appreciation of technology as well as history and art.

For one thing, even as they continued to churn out their engravings of the battles and leaders of the Civil War, newspaper critics—and their audiences—found the newer-fangled marvels of the infant medium of photography understandably more compelling. Woodcuts made for the picture press from hasty battlefield sketches looked and felt ephemeral; they were examined week by week, but seldom preserved, much less displayed. Many of the engravings and lithographs published specifically for parlor display, often in rich colors, nonetheless looked one-dimensional, rote, romanticized, and amateurish. It was often difficult, for example, through the details of terrain or portraiture, to distinguish one battle from another in these prints. Newfangled carte-de-visite photographs, however, perfectly captured the new spirit of grim realism that engulfed America. The first display of dead bodies on the battlefield, in an 1862 New York exhibition of photographs by Mathew Brady entitled *The Dead of Antietam,* caused a sensation. Moreover, any American could own a photograph and keep it in a family album. Paintings remained more remote—products of imagination and talent, but available to few.

It is important to remember that the now-familiar idea of the public art museum, where people of all classes could examine and appreciate paintings, was largely a postwar phenomenon. The Metropolitan Museum of Art did not open its doors until 1872; the Art Institute of Chicago opened in 1879. Until then, the only way large masses of people could see paintings—of peace or war—was at brief special exhibitions at galleries, fairs, or cycloramas, impermanent temporary events, not permanent testimony to the enduring power of the finest works of art.

During the war, art had been displayed at Northern "Sanitary Fairs" devoted to selling artifacts for the benefit of the soldiers. In 1865, a smattering of Civil War paintings at a local exhibit at the city's National Academy of Design was enough to inspire one visitor—a frustrated novelist and poet—to undertake a new volume of verse. The result was an immortal collection called *Battle-Pieces*. The writer's name was Herman Melville, and Civil War art had inspired him back into print. But it was not until 1867 that New York City hosted its first exhibition devoted exclusively to "Pictures of the War."

When art was seen, there was no denying its power. When John Antrobus's portrait of Grant went on display in the U.S. Capitol in 1864, for example, it unleashed a sensation. The painting inspired no less a spectator than Lincoln himself, who had yet to meet the general face to face, to personally go and see it for himself—if only, some whispered, to take the measure of the man who might be challenging the president for the Republican nomination that year.

And when William D. Washington's *Burial of Latane* went on view on the streets of Richmond in 1865—a rather stilted canvas (by today's standards) showing a woman preaching a funeral service for a Confederate officer on her plantation, with women, children, and loyal slaves looking on—it caused such a sensation that impoverished residents of the ruined city threw coins and jewelry into a nearby pail to aid wounded soldiers.

Not everyone appreciated these early efforts to consecrate the war pictorially. They could arouse controversy and resentment, too. When in 1870 Peter F. Rothermel unveiled his colossal painting of the Confederate high-water mark at Gettysburg—paid for by the State of Pennsylvania— Gen. George G. Meade commented: "This is not a picture only—it is an epic—a national struggle, a national record." But Lost Cause sympathizers found the painting deeply offensive, complaining that "the face of every dying Union soldier is lighted up with a celestial smile, while guilt and despair are stamped on the wan countenances of the moribund rebels." Pictures that appear today to be mere battlefield vistas once evoked bitter disputes over their subtle but undeniable points of view.

Sometimes, their impact relied solely on spectacle. When the gigantic Gettysburg Cyclorama opened in Boston in 1884, a critic marveled that it was "as though the laws of this world were suspended." Audiences flocked to see it with the same passion for wide-eyed wonder that today attracts moviegoers to high-tech animated wonders like *Avatar.*

Eventually, artists did give the Civil War serious and imaginative appraisal in such large quantities of work that no historian has yet attempted, much less succeeded, in calculating their number. Museums opened to the public and gave audiences a permanent place to contemplate art from around the world—including the art of the recent, convulsive war. Postwar artists like Winslow Homer and Gilbert Gaul reinvigorated interest in the conflict with canvases that were, respectively, perceptive and dramatic. It was enough, at last, for the *New York Tribune* to proclaim: "Art has gained some good even from 'the struggle.'"

History gained some good, too. For over the years, the notion that Civil War art serves merely as illustration for the written word has slowly vanished—thanks to the determination and talent of artists spanning the generations. Few have shown more skill, attention to accuracy, and reverence for the past than Mort Künstler. During the Civil War, the idea of a book devoted entirely to pictures by a single artist would have been inconceivable. Now, this thirteenth book of Künstler's Civil War paintings not only seems a natural and appealing means to historical memory, but takes its rightful place in Civil War literature and memory. And it helps correct the long-held misunderstanding of the tradition and considerable impact of military art.

What was said 150 years ago about one of the finest of the nineteenth-century artists to focus on the Civil War— Sanford Gifford—might be said with entire confidence of Künstler: "His best pictures can be not only merely seen but contemplated with entire satisfaction; they indicate a capacity based upon genuine principles."

—HAROLD HOLZER

INTRODUCTION

THE CIVIL WAR ABIDES DEEP in the American soul, and so long as there is a United States it will not go away. Nor should it. The war is not some closed chapter in our dusty past. It is the high-water mark of our national history: the starting point from which we measure the dimensions of just about everything that has happened to us since.

Growing pains are integral steps to maturity. That applies to countries as well as to individuals. The American nation created in 1787 mushroomed in the decades thereafter. It was a time of great growth and energy. From the seed-bed of thirteen colonies huddled along the Atlantic coast, the country's boundaries steadily moved westward three thousand miles. Millions of immigrants poured into the cities of the East, while millions of residents headed west in search of gold and richer lands. Unfocused vitality made growth erratic. No centrality existed to it all.

Economics in the first half of the nineteenth century was likewise unbalanced. The leading product was Southern cotton. It required both land that growers were always seeking and cheap labor supplied by black slaves. By mid-century, South Carolina's senator James Hammond could shout: "The slaveholding South is now the controlling power of the world! . . . Cotton is king!" Sectionalism by areas, politics, and social levels became inevitable.

That same era (1820–60) gave rise to numerous humanitarian movements associated with growth. Ralph Waldo Emerson exulted: "What a fertility of projects for the salvation of the world!" Robert Lowell observed with more restraint that "all stood ready at a moment's notice to reform everything but themselves."

Soon, one movement—the abolition of slavery—dwarfed the other reforms. Slavery seemed to be the evil that most violated democratic institutions. Beginning in 1831, an abolitionist crusade grew with each passing year. Such a movement was a direct threat to cotton planters who made their fortunes from slave labor.

Americans on both sides of the Potomac River came more and more to emphasize their differences rather than their similarities. The ill feeling of the 1830s became the arguments of the 1840s, then the shouting of the 1850s. American presidents after Andrew Jackson and before Abraham Lincoln were mediocre at best. The Congress talked much, said little, and did nothing. The seventy-year experiment in democracy collapsed.

Beginning in 1860, South Carolina led an exodus of seven states from the Union. That bloc created the Confederate States of America and asked only to be left alone. Newly inaugurated president Abraham Lincoln had no intention of allowing such a situation. The nation that would stand passively by and watch itself disintegrate, Lincoln believed, was unworthy of the name.

In the next four years, the Civil War became America's most profound experience, second only to the winning of independence. Three million young men from North and South disliked danger and hardship as much as anyone. Yet their "country" needed them, and no matter what it asked, they felt an obligation to answer the call. What those Johnny Rebs and Billy Yanks did—the lives they lived, the memories they recounted, the sacrifices they made, the deaths they died—this is all part of our national evolution. It should be as real to us as the events of last week.

This book is a memorial to those who fought—and to those who continue to fight—for the American dream.

We are one nation because good men of North and South who fought for God-given beliefs molded us into one. That is an overriding remembrance that must always prevail.

Mort Künstler has truly kept that faith during a life of achievement.

He is the foremost Civil War artist of our time (if not of all time) because of his devotion to truth and detail in history. No one has better captured on

Confederate Christmas

canvas the sights, the feelings, the encompassing drama that formed the conflict of the 1860s. Many gifted wielders of the brush have given us scores of Civil War illustrations, but only Künstler has carried that skill to a level approaching perfection.

To study his paintings is simply to see history alive. Famous generals stand in poses as noble as they are endearing. Johnny Rebs and Billy Yanks, inspiring representatives of America's common folk, show their courage in battle, their endurance in the field, and their dedication to the generals who controlled their lives. And no lover of animals can view a Künstler painting without marveling at the beauty and realism of the horses. All the ingredients of war and life carefully adorn every Mort Künstler creation.

—James I. Robertson Jr.

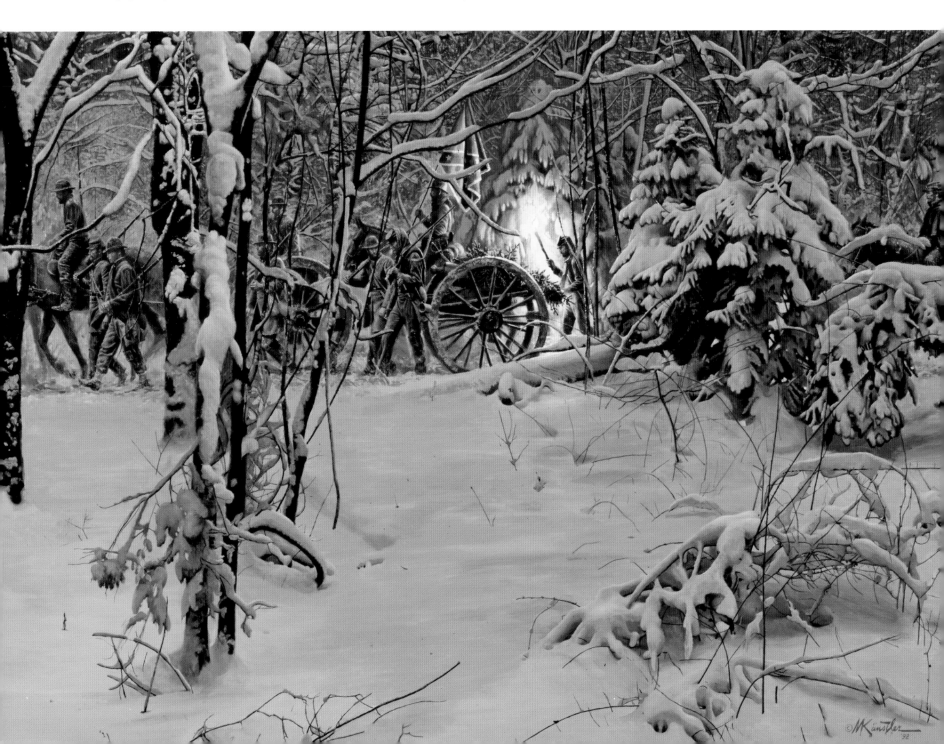

CHAPTER ONE

COLLAPSE OF A NATION

1850s

IN 1858, THREE YEARS BEFORE CIVIL war exploded, a small-town Georgia editor saw it coming. Catastrophe was unavoidable, he believed. "Every day, week, month and year brings an increasing alienation of feeling between [North and South]. . . . Disunion will come . . . as the inevitable fruition of an uncompromising hatred, rankling and deepening through years of insult and wrong, itself a result of the belief that it can be *safely* inflicted."

Disagreement over the issue of slavery had been loud and unchecked for twenty-five years prior to the editor's lament. Debates intensified in spring of 1846 with the declaration of war with Mexico (a Southern attempt to gain more cotton fields, abolitionists charged). The Mexican War quickly produced the Wilmot Proviso in Congress, banning slavery in any Mexican territory acquired by the United States. Slavery now came to the forefront of American politics and remained the overwhelming issue for fourteen years, until South Carolina led the progress of secession.

The 1850s was a decade in which one event piled atop the smoking heap of another. The heat intensified until it became unbearable.

On September 4, Congress passed the Compromise of 1850. The two key clauses of the package of bills were the admission of California as a free state (thereby ending the senatorial balance between Northern and Southern states) and a new, stringent fugitive slave act that empowered federal agents to chase runaway slaves and return them to their masters.

After the compromise proved little more than an armistice, Harriet Beecher Stowe published her incendiary *Uncle Tom's Cabin* (1852). The novel clearly declared slavery immoral *and* unchristian. Angry Southern writers responded with a half-dozen "Uncle Tom" books of their own.

A NATION-BUILDING IDEA of a transcontinental railroad got nowhere thanks to heated jockeying over whether the eastern terminus of the line would be in a Southern or Northern city. This impasse led to the 1854 Kansas-Nebraska Act, which produced open fighting between pro-slave and anti-slave factions in what became known as "Bleeding Kansas." In the midst of this dispute, Rep. Preston Brooks of South Carolina physically assaulted Sen. Charles Sumner in

"**Every day,** week, month and year brings an **increasing alienation** of feeling between [North and South].... **Disunion will come.**"

—*The Georgia Telegraph,* 1858

the Capitol. The "Bully Brooks Affair" clearly showed that emotion was replacing reason.

In 1857 the Supreme Court entered the fray with a decision (*Dred Scott v. Sandford*) pronouncing that black slaves, and their descendents, were not citizens but private property. The high court's decision, among other firebombs, brought into question the status of a quarter-million freedmen in America.

Attention in the 1858 off-year elections turned to Illinois, where a powerful Democrat, Stephen A. Douglas, sought reelection to the U.S. Senate. He faced Republican opposition from a relatively unknown candidate named Abraham Lincoln. Their debates, reported across the nation, underscored the schism in thinking between free and slave territory. When abolitionist John Brown the following year seized the federal arsenal at Harpers Ferry, Virginia, in a bloody insurrection to free slaves, the nation seemed to have reached a point from which it could not turn back.

The last shreds of national unity crumbled during the 1860 presidential election. Abraham Lincoln edged out victory over three opponents. His Republican platform was against any extension of slavery in the United States. Politically, economically, socially, "the will of the people" left the Southern states with nowhere to go inside the Union.

On December 20, South Carolina became the first of seven states to secede. Staunch Unionist James L. Petigru in Charleston sneered that an independent South Carolina would never survive. "South Carolina," he said, "is too small to be a nation, and too large to be an insane asylum."

A "Confederate States of America" was established in mid-February 1861. Jefferson Davis of Mississippi and Alexander H. Stephens of Georgia became president and vice president, respectively.

The nation's leaders had spent the 1850s repeatedly stretching democratic perimeters to the breaking point, everyone confident that the system would tolerate the blows and repair itself. Reasonable people went to unreasonable limits. They talked; soon they threatened; and all the ingredients of compromise that had held democracy together evaporated. The great American undertaking, bloated with turmoil, broke apart from intolerance. The future was invisible, because the past had been a failure.

Beginnings in New Salem

Several members of the Lincoln family in Virginia's Shenandoah Valley headed west to find a new life in the expanding nation. Thomas Lincoln was one of them. In 1831 his twenty-two-year-old son Abraham—a "friendless, uneducated, penniless boy," as he called himself—was a storekeeper in the village of New Salem, Illinois.

Tall, craggy, and awkward, Lincoln was hardworking and ambitious. He was hardly a refined gentleman, but no one who ever saw him would fail to take a second look.

A New Salem resident once asked Lincoln what he would do if he had money. Lincoln replied that he would like to study law.

Lincoln, the Family Man

Lincoln moved to Springfield, Illinois, in 1836, to begin a law practice, and married Mary Todd six years later. They had four sons, yet Robert, the oldest, would be the only one to survive into adulthood.

The Lincoln—Douglas Debates

Ottawa, Illinois, August 21, 1858 *(opposite)*

In 1858 Sen. Stephen A. Douglas stood for reelection in Illinois. The new Republican Party nominated a dark horse: Abraham Lincoln. The rawboned Lincoln was a physical contrast to his suave and polished opponent, and he knew it. Douglas once referred to Lincoln as a two-faced man. Quickly Lincoln asked his audience: "If I had two faces, do you think I would wear this one in public?"

Douglas considered slavery a local issue whose expansion rested on popular sovereignty—the theory that the people of a territory by themselves had the right to determine whether they entered the Union as a free or slave state. A major theme in Lincoln's campaign was his now-famous statement made when he accepted the Republican nomination: "A house divided against itself cannot stand. I believe the government cannot endure half slave and half free."

Lincoln lost the senatorial election but gained national prominence by his oratory and anti-expansion views.

The Professor from Maine

Joshua L. Chamberlain at Bowdoin College

His parents wanted Joshua Lawrence Chamberlain to enter the ministry. Yet in the 1850s the mild-mannered scholar taught rhetoric and modern languages at Bowdoin College in Maine. Chamberlain was familiar with, and sympathetic to, abolitionists through his friendship with Harriet Beecher Stowe and her activist family. He came to believe that a system "so repugnant to justice and freedom as that of slavery should be limited, not extended—repressed, not encouraged; and that some way should be found to . . . wipe that blot off from our escutcheon."

Chamberlain's love of country was rooted deeply in the stony ground of New England.

The Professor from Virginia

Thomas J. Jackson at Virginia Military Institute

An orphan from the mountains of western Virginia, Thomas J. Jackson graduated from West Point, fought heroically in the Mexican War, and in 1851 joined the faculty at Virginia Military Institute as a professor of natural and experimental philosophy. He was such a demanding teacher that cadets labeled him "Tom Fool," "Old Blue Light," and "Hell and Thunder."

Jackson too had a deep love of country. By the end of the 1850s, his second wife Anna noted, Jackson believed "that the constitutional rights of the States had been invaded, and he never had a doubt as to where his allegiance was due. His sword belonged to his State."

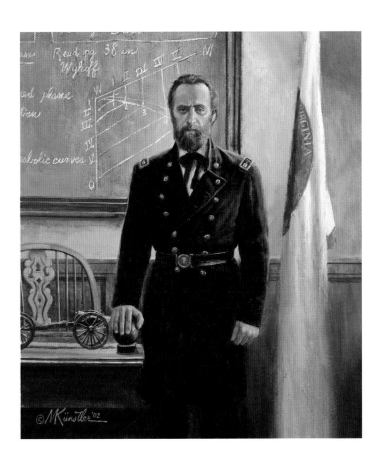

CHAPTER TWO

UNCERTAINTIES OF WAR

1861

WARFARE BEGAN IN A WEIRD WAY. It was as if the two sides doubted the determination of each other and then stumbled into a collision over a trifle, which mushroomed into a full-scale fight that neither side seemed to grasp clearly.

Armed conflict was a natural result of secession. In the departed states were federal properties: military posts, arsenals, and post offices. Confederate states, exerting their newfound sovereignty, demanded the surrender of all federal installations. Most local officials (Southerners themselves) readily consented.

The eighty-four-man garrison at Fort Sumter did not. A pentagon of masonry situated on an artificial island in the center of Charleston harbor, the fort was hardly a threat to the Southern government. Yet the American flag flying over Fort Sumter was an insult to the sovereign state of South Carolina. Confederates began positioning artillery around three sides of the fort.

When Lincoln announced early in April 1861 that he was humanely sending food (not ammunition) to the besieged garrison, this move struck many as throwing down the gauntlet. On April 12, Confederates responded by opening fire on Sumter with over forty guns.

An undercurrent of chivalry prevailed throughout the thirty-four-hour bombardment. At one point, wooden portions of the fort caught fire. Confederates ceased the barrage and inquired politely if the Federals needed aid in extinguishing the flames. The one-sided, bloodless bombardment ended when the fort's commander crawled through the debris and waved a white flag. As Union soldiers departed by ship from Charleston, Southern troops along the coast saluted.

Fort Sumter brought North and South to war. At the outset, Confederates committed two fatal errors in judgment. Men like Jefferson Davis firmly believed secession to be a constitutional right of a state. Southern leaders were also convinced that Northerners would not fight to preserve a Union that obviously had failed. On the other hand, Lincoln considered the United States to be indissoluble. The actions of the Deep South states were therefore misguided rebellion. On the fifteenth, Lincoln issued a call for 75,000 volunteer soldiers to put down the Confederate uprising. This attempt at coercion sent four more states (Virginia, Tennessee, North Carolina, and Arkansas) into the Confederate fold.

Eleven Southern states now faced nineteen Northern states with a four-to-one superiority in manpower. War fever became a national epidemic. Georgian Hiram Barclay recalled: "It seemed to me that the people were crazy and we were wild crazy." A Richmond visitor, J. T. Smith, observed: "Virginia is all ablaze and Lincoln will never wave the scepter of despotism over the sons of the Old Dominion."

The Northern call to arms took on a personal meaning. People who were not stunned were apprehensive or—in most cases—infuriated by the firing on Fort Sumter. Oliver Wendell Holmes wrote angrily: "The first gun that spat its iron insult at Fort Sumter, smote every loyal American full in the face." On April 15 the *New York Times* wrote: "The President's Proclamation will be hailed with an enthusiasm which no event of the last twenty years has brought forth,—with a high-hearted determination to exterminate treason, which will carry terror into the hearts of the Confederates." In Milwaukee, a judge and jury left the courtroom and enlisted as a group.

Johnny Rebs and Billy Yanks alike left for war with youthful eagerness to defend their country and loved ones. A great adventure lay ahead. Soldiers were going to fight because they wanted to fight; and in their innocence they did not have the remotest idea what the reality would be. All had fanciful ideas of departing as soldiers and returning as heroes.

To restore the Union, Federal armies would have to take the offensive. Virginia, directly across the Potomac River from the national capital, was the first and obvious avenue of invasion. The mountainous western counties of the state had never had much in common with the tidewater elitists, so when Virginia left the Union, westerners began talking about leaving Virginia. Union troops moved into the northern tier of those counties in order to protect the Baltimore & Ohio Railroad, Washington's sole link with the country beyond the mountains. In due course, Virginia Unionists in the mountains would organize their own state of West Virginia.

For three months after Fort Sumter, both sides pursued chaotic mobilization for war. The Union army in 1861 numbered 16,000 men scattered all over the country. A Confederate army did not exist. Organizing, learning, drilling, gathering arms and supplies all took time. Meanwhile, politicians and the press clamored constantly for the one battle that would convince the other side to see the evil of its ways and quit.

A Union effort to advance westward from Fort Monroe up the Virginia peninsula failed after a sharp little fight at Big Bethel on June 10. Some 15,000 Federal recruits under venerable Gen. Robert Patterson massed around Harpers Ferry near the northern entrance to the Shenandoah Valley. They were too ineptly led to be a serious threat. The major Union effort would come out of Washington; the plan was to seize control of two rail lines converging at Manassas Junction and then march triumphantly to the Confederate capital at Richmond.

That Union force of 35,000 inexperienced troops was twice the size of any army ever mustered in North America. It was under the command of Gen. Irvin McDowell, who had been a major and staff officer three months earlier. McDowell knew that his regiments were not ready for action, but public pressure was overwhelming.

Guarding Manassas Junction were 22,000 equally green recruits under Fort Sumter victor Gustave Beauregard. Another 10,000 Southerners, led by Gen. Joseph E. Johnston, were sixty miles to the west at Winchester in the Shenandoah Valley. When McDowell's columns began lurching forward into Virginia, Johnston gave Patterson the slip and transferred his men by rail and road to reinforce Beauregard.

Southern strength along Bull Run was now equal to that of the Federals. That gave the defense the decided advantage in battle. However, the July 21 clash at Manassas was not a normal battle. It was a collision between two armed mobs. Inexperience was evident throughout the fighting, especially with the attacking Federals. A New Hampshire soldier wrote disgustedly: "Every order was a blunder and every movement a failure."

Officers could only point men toward the action and hope for the best. The intensity of the battle itself was a shock to the farmers, clerks, and students who filled the ranks. Confederate Thomas Perry stated in wonder: "It was one continual thunder upon thunder until the Earth seemed to shake its very foundations."

A sudden, bold counterattack by a brigade under the command of a Virginia Military Institute professor won the day and sent Federals scurrying in near-panic back to Washington. Casualties in what became known as First Bull Run or First Manassas were 868 killed and 2,583 wounded. This was a small fight by the standards of later engagements. Still, Manassas was the largest and bloodiest battle the nation had ever known.

Another Confederate success, far to the west, came the next month. Two equally unseasoned armies battled at Wilson's Creek, Missouri, for control of the state. The Southern victory was short-lived.

Lincoln made it clear that this was not going to be "a one-battle war" when he issued a summer call for 500,000 additional volunteers. While too many Southerners rested on their laurels, new Union regiments arrived in Washington during August and September at the rate of 15,000 men a week. A new, charismatic general named George B. McClellan began creating a massive force he called the Army of the Potomac. High morale came with intense training. "The boys are as happy as clams at high water," a Massachusetts soldier wrote home that autumn. "The rank and file think that [McClellan] is just the man to lead us to victory."

Confederate officials focused on strengthening defenses. President Davis dispatched his military adviser, Gen. Robert E. Lee, to Charleston to make a stronger bastion of that port. As a reward for heroism at Manassas, Gen. Thomas "Stonewall" Jackson was assigned command of the agriculturally rich and militarily strategic Shenandoah Valley. Meanwhile, the *Daily Richmond Examiner* was reassuring its readers: "The enemy must be made to feel the war. They must be made to understand that there is a God that punishes the wicked, and that the Southern army is His instrument."

"The enemy must be made to feel the war. They must be made to understand that there is a God that punishes the wicked, and that the Southern army is His instrument."

—*Daily Richmond Examiner,* September 24, 1861

Florida Secedes

January 10, 1861 *(left)*

The third of the first seven states to leave the Union was Florida. Since the state was essentially an extension of Georgia and Alabama, its exodus in January 1861 was no surprise.

In 1861, Florida's population was less than that of the city of New Orleans. Forty percent of the residents were slaves. Salt and cattle became its chief material contributions to the Confederacy. Of 15,000 Floridians who entered the army, a third died in service.

Florida governor John Milton could not endure defeat. On April 1, 1865, he committed suicide. However, most war-weary Floridians shared the feelings of a returning veteran: "Thank God, it is over, one way or the other."

The Great Decision

Robert E. Lee, April 1861 *(right)*

Winfield Scott, general-in-chief of the U.S. Army until 1861, considered Lee—who had served under him in the Mexican-American War—the best soldier in the army. Robert E. Lee had given more than thirty years of distinguished service to the nation. Deeper than that, however, he was a Virginian.

The Civil War was only hours old when Lee was offered command of the main Union army to be assembled at Washington. Lee vividly recalled that his father, Gen. Henry "Light Horse Harry" Lee, had faced the same personal crisis years earlier during debates over states' rights spurred by the Kentucky and Virginia resolutions of 1798–99. Henry Lee had then declared: "Virginia is my country. Her will I obey, however lamentable the fate to which it may subject me." Robert Lee considered slavery "a moral & political evil." Secession, he thought, was "nothing but revolution." Yet Federal forces would be invading Virginia. "I cannot raise my hand against my birthplace, my home, my children," Lee declared.

It was not that he loved America less, but that he loved Virginia more. The fifty-four-year-old soldier resigned from the U.S. Army. "Save in defense of my native state," he said, "I never desire again to draw my sword."

"The air was so pure and fragrant that **its inhalation**

was a positive **luxury."**

——Eliza McHatton-Ripley

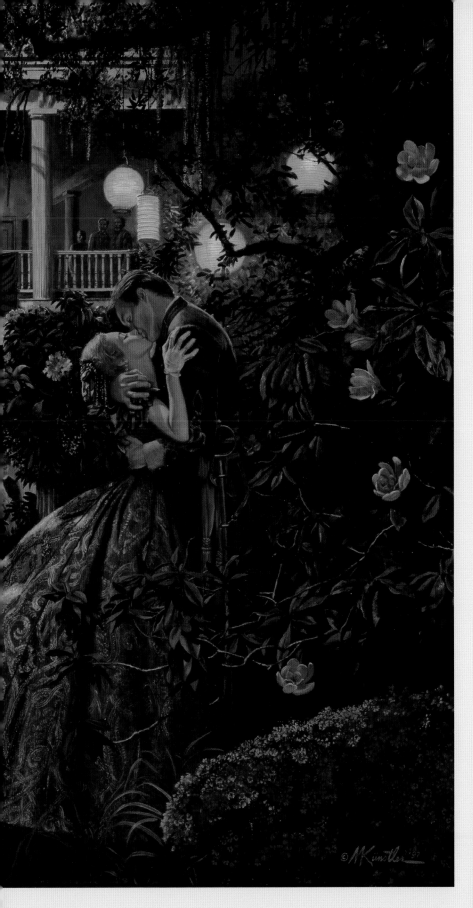

Moonlight and Magnolias
The Stolen Kiss *(study, below)*

Arlington Plantation, Lake Providence, Louisiana, April 6–7, 1861

"ARLINGTON" was the Louisiana plantation of attorney Edward Sparrow, who purchased the property in 1852. The plantation was at Lake Providence in the northeastern corner of the state. Sparrow would become a member of the Confederate States Senate and chair of the powerful Committee on Military Affairs. Before a shot had been fired, Sparrow hosted a grand ball on April 6, 1861, in honor of the Confederacy. Guests from as far away as New Orleans and Baton Rouge traveled across the state for the event. On spring evenings such as this, Eliza McHatton-Ripley later recalled, "the air was so pure and fragrant that its inhalation was a positive luxury."

From the upstairs porch railing hung (*left to right* here, and in *Magnolia Morning* on the following pages) the new Louisiana state flag adopted two weeks earlier, the first national "Stars and Bars" flag of the Confederacy, and the pelican flag used by Louisiana prior to secession. It was too early in the war for standardization of uniforms. Thus, well-equipped Louisiana officers were in a wide variety of dress.

Mrs. McHatton later wrote, "We did not, in fact could not, realize the mightiness of the impending future." Revelry and romance marked the evening as everyone enjoyed the novel excitement of war.

The mansion survived the destruction of war largely because some of Union general U. S. Grant's staff officers lived there during the 1863 Vicksburg campaign. Today Arlington is the last of the great antebellum homes in the Lake Providence area.

"**We** did not, in fact

could not, realize

the mightiness

of the impending **future.**"

——Eliza McHatton-Ripley

Magnolia Morning

The Flag and Union Imperiled

Charleston, South Carolina, April 12–13, 1861

The Confederate fire from Fort Moultrie on the northern face of Sumter was especially damaging. Inside the besieged garrison, Sgt. John Carmody was furious that Sumter—undermanned, and with its heaviest guns on the exposed parapet—was undergoing intense bombardment and Union soldiers could not return the fire. Knowing that the heavy guns on the barbette deck were loaded, primed, and aimed, Carmody sneaked away from his post, climbed the ramparts, and—one by one—fired every gun pointed toward Moultrie. "The contest was merely Carmody against the Confederate States," fellow Sgt. John Chester stated. Carmody then returned to his station, "not because he was beaten, but because he was unable, single-handed, to reload his guns."

No one mentioned Carmody's heroic deed in official reports of the engagement, but Maj. Anderson declared: "The officers and men of my command acquitted themselves in a manner which entitled them to the thanks and gratitude of their country."

Fort Sumter, First Shot

Charleston, South Carolina, April 12, 1861

Fort Sumter had been under construction for thirty-two years when it became the center of national attention. Although the bastion had three floors and was sixty feet in height, only 15 of the planned 135 guns were in place.

During the April 12–13 bombardment, Confederates fired 3,000 shots at the fort. Most of the shells came from light-caliber guns. Not one penetrated the five-foot-thick walls. Some shells arched over the walls into the fort. Barracks and anything else wooden in the interior eventually caught fire. A Charleston observer commented later that the bombardment made Sumter look like it had a serious case of smallpox.

Inside the fort, the Union defenders experienced quite different feelings. Pvt. James Thompson never forgot the helpless experience. "Something like an expression of awe came over the features of everyone as battery after battery opened fire and the hissing shot came plowing along leaving wreck and ruin in their path."

Gen. Pierre Gustave Toutant Beauregard ordered the first shot.

Gen. P. G. T. Beauregard

Louisiana

In command of the Confederate fire was the dark-haired, olive-skinned Gen. P. G. T. Beauregard of Louisiana. He was a contentious officer given to Napoleonic poses and grandiose strategy. Most of the soldiers admired him. Yet Jefferson Davis was so offended by Beauregard's flamboyance that when he found a showy officer and did not know what to do with him, he assigned him to the Louisianan's staff.

Beauregard was somewhat subdued at Fort Sumter, in part because he had studied artillery tactics at West Point under Maj. Robert Anderson, who commanded the Sumter garrison.

Sumter's fall would bring extravagant praise of Beauregard throughout the Confederacy. One popular piece of doggerel went: "With cannon and musket, with shell and petard / We salute the North with our Beauregard."

Mary Anna and Thomas J. Jackson

Lexington, Virginia, April 1861

During his years at Virginia Military Institute (VMI) as a natural philosophy (physics) professor, Maj. Thomas Jackson had two wives. The first, Elinor Junkin, died in childbirth in 1854, fourteen months after their wedding. Three years later, in 1857, Jackson married Mary Anna Morrison (known as Anna). Their union lasted six years until his death.

Both wives were daughters of Presbyterian ministers. Both taught Jackson how to be outgoing and cordial. With both, he shared a deep religious faith. Reading the Bible together was a daily occurrence.

The prospect of civil war did not bother the professor. "Why should Christians be disturbed about the dissolution of the Union?" he asked. "It can come only by God's permission, and will only be permitted if for His people's good; for does He not say, 'All things work together to them that love God?'"

Maj. Thomas J. Jackson Leaves VMI *(study, left)* · Road to Glory *(above)*

Lexington, Virginia, April 21, 1861

Three days after Virginia's secession, VMI superintendent Francis Smith received orders from Gov. John Letcher to send the bulk of the corps of cadets to Richmond. They were to act as drillmasters for the stream of recruits pouring into the capital. Col. Smith assigned Maj. Thomas Jackson to be in charge of the transfer.

Sunday, April 21, was a quiet morning in Lexington. At his home, Jackson knelt with his wife and prayed that "if consistent with His will, God would still avert the threatening danger and grant us peace."

At 12:30 p.m., clad in his blue faculty uniform, Jackson led 176 cadets and eight officers down the hill from the Institute. Maj. Raleigh Colston, the mounted officer behind Jackson, was struck by the changes in his friend's usually subdued countenance. Jackson's "speech quickened, his eyes glittered, his drowsy manner had left him, and his whole nature seemed to wake up."

The white VMI flag was carried in front of the marching cadets. Murray Taylor, a younger cadet left behind, wrote of his departing classmates: "They represented many of the best and most famous families of Virginia and the Southern States."

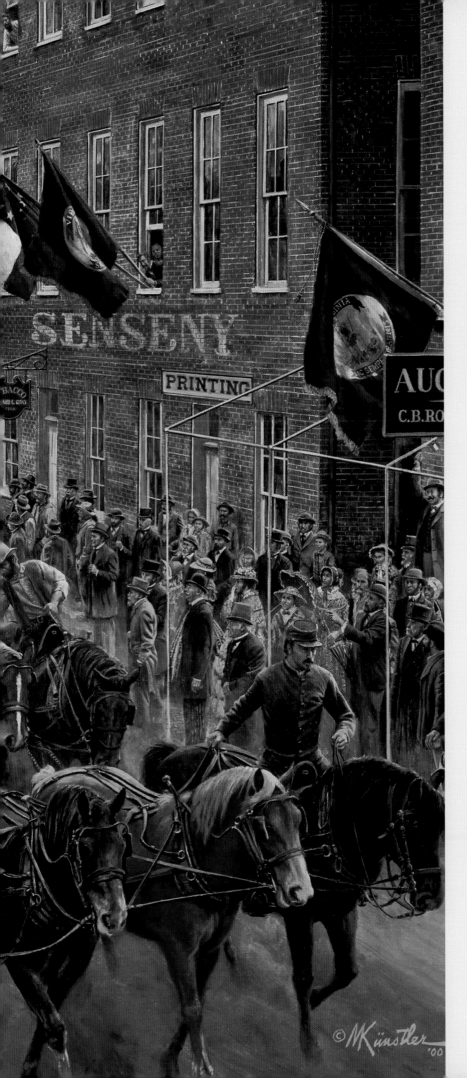

Iron Horses, Men of Steel

Winchester, Virginia, June 1861

Jackson Commandeers the Railroad

Martinsburg, Virginia, June 1861 (*following pages*)

In mid-June, Thomas Jackson, now a colonel, and his five regiments of Shenandoah Valley troops—awaiting their first military action in Winchester, Virginia—received instructions to proceed twenty miles to Martinsburg. There they were to destroy the extensive shops and stock of the Baltimore & Ohio Railroad. Jackson knew how badly the South needed railroad engines. "It was sad work," he wrote his wife, "but I had my orders and my duty was to obey."

In addition to burning the main station, roundhouse, and machine shops, fifty-six locomotives and tenders and 305 gondola cars loaded with coal were put to the torch. As he watched the destruction, Jackson developed a plan for salvaging the least damaged locomotives and transporting them to the railhead at Strasburg, thirty-eight miles away.

The colonel selected thirteen locomotives. Mechanics dismantled the engines. Wheel trucks, piston rails, valves, bell, whistle—every pound of weight that could be removed from the boilers was placed on wagons with wooden wheels. Meanwhile, officers and teamsters collected workhorses, mules, and thorough-breds in the region for the forty-horse pulling power that each locomotive would require. The horses were rigged four abreast and driven by riders controlling four horses each. Some owners refused to part with their animals unless they could drive them personally.

When all of the complicated assembly was ready, the Trojan warhorse spectacle began the slow journey to Strasburg. Dust swirled; teams balked; every bridge and any pit of size became obstacles. Close to 200 men "added their muscle, their shouts, their curses and wild singing to the racket." The trip required three days, allowing for rest and breakdowns of various sorts. Although Jackson had watched carefully over every preparatory detail, he was attending to other duty when the procession passed through Winchester. Crowds of curious and awed onlookers watched the strange train pass through.

This joint military-civilian operation was Jackson's idea. It became a model thereafter for the overland shipping of railroad rolling stock.

Victory Rode the Rails

Jackson at Piedmont Station,
July 19, 1861

Jackson's 1st Brigade was the van of 12,000 Confederate troops who left Winchester to reinforce Beauregard at Manassas. For a day and a half, the men struggled across streams and over a mountain range. Early on July 19, they reached Piedmont Station, where they would board Manassas Gap Railroad trains for the thirty-four-mile trip to the battle line. Capt. James Edmondson of the 4th Virginia sent a quick note to his wife: "Here we are after a forced march, nearly broken down and without anything to eat."

Local residents rushed to feed the soldiers. When the first train of cattle cars arrived for loading, Daniel Conrad of the 2nd Virginia noted: "we packed ourselves like so many pins and needles, and, as safety for engine and cars was more essential than speed. . . . We slowly jolted the entire day."

Jackson, in the center of the painting, is conferring with aide Alexander "Sandie" Pendleton and surgeon Hunter McGuire. The train station building in the background still stands.

Crowds cheered the trains all along the way, "with showers of bouquets and kisses thrown by the fairer sex," a soldier added. Going to war seemed glorious.

"There Stands Jackson Like a Stone Wall"

General Thomas J. Jackson at First Manassas, July 21, 1861 (*below*)
"THERE STANDS JACKSON LIKE A STONE WALL" (*study, right*)

It was the critical moment in the all-day battle on the plains of Manassas. Federal troops had pounded the left flank of the Southern position for hours. The line finally broke, fragments of units falling back toward Henry House Hill, the geographical key to the whole battleground.

Unknown to everyone involved in the fighting, Gen. Thomas Jackson had placed his five regiments out of sight behind the crest of the hill. Union artillery raked the area for over two hours. Jackson periodically called out: "Steady, men, steady! All's well!"

Just as the retreating Confederates reached the base of Henry House Hill, Jackson ordered his brigade into position on the hilltop. Gen. Barnard Bee of South Carolina had attended West Point with the Virginian. When he saw the new battle line in place, Bee shouted in a booming voice: "Look, men! There is Jackson standing like a stone wall! Let us determine to die here, and we will conquer!"

The Virginians sent a concentrated volley of musketry into the advancing Union line. A 79th New York soldier wrote: "The first fire swept our ranks like a quick darting pestilence." Jackson's men, screaming loudly, then charged into the disjointed Federals. Fighting raged over the hillside for almost an hour before Union troops began withdrawing from the entire field.

Barnard Bee that day gave the Southern cause not only his life but also the most famous nickname in American military history.

"Get up, **Louisianans! Charge them!** Do you all want to be killed?"

—Col. James McIntosh

First to the Guns

Battle of Wilson's Creek, August 10, 1861

The first major test of arms in the land beyond the Mississippi River came on August 10, 1861, in southwestern Missouri. Impetuous Union general Nathaniel Lyon attacked a large Confederate force under Gen. Ben McCulloch at Wilson's Creek, a small stream about twelve miles from Springfield.

Union fire soon had the 3rd Louisiana pinned down. "Men were dropping all over the line," a private stated. Col. James McIntosh of McCulloch's staff came galloping down the line.

"Get up, Louisianans!" he yelled. "Charge them! Do you all want to be killed?"

Reinforced by an Arkansas regiment, the 3rd Louisiana swept forward under its unique pelican flag and overran a Union battery. This was the unit's first fight, Col. Louis Hebert reported, and McIntosh "greatly contributed to the success of our arms."

McIntosh died a year later while leading a similar charge at Pea Ridge, Arkansas.

"The Sweetest Music . . ."

Gen. Stonewall Jackson, November 4, 1861

Early in November, Jackson received promotion to major general and orders to take charge of all defenses in the Shenandoah Valley. The one bad aspect of the assignment was saying goodbye to the "Stonewall Brigade," to which he had given life and fame.

"The scene was very effecting indeed," Capt. James Edmondson of the 27th Virginia admitted. The brigade stood at attention in close regimental file. Jackson looked slowly along the ranks. Both men and general were having a problem controlling their emotion. Lips quivering, Jackson told the soldiers of the acclaim they had won and the "imperishable honor" they had gained at Manassas. Then Jackson removed his cap, stood in the stirrups, and exclaimed loudly: "In the future, on the fields on which the Stonewall Brigade are engaged, I expect to hear of crowning deeds of valor and of victories gloriously achieved! May God bless you all! Farewell!"

He galloped off to a deafening roar from the men. Amid the shouts echoed the rebel yell, which they had created and which Jackson thought "the sweetest music I ever heard." The yell was a totally uncoordinated, high-pitched scream of one-syllable sounds (*yi-yi-yi, who-who-who*) with no two being similar. Coming from thousands of charging soldiers, the yell was meant to be more intimidating than inspirational. Hearing it, one Federal remembered, "made the hair stand up on my head." Another Billy Yank referred to it as "that terrible scream and barbarous howling."

Charleston—Autumn 1861

Gen. Robert E. Lee at the Mills House, Charleston, South Carolina

Robert E. Lee was President Davis's military adviser and one of five full generals in Confederate service. Longing for field duty, Lee instead was sent in November 1861 to command a new coastal department of South Carolina, Georgia, and eastern Florida. His ticklish tasks were to persuade state-minded governors to send more troops to Virginia while shoring up their defenses along the Atlantic shore.

Lee's rank and position entitled him to high courtesy. In Charleston he was a guest at the prestigious Mills House. As Lee watched the relaxed street atmosphere from the hotel balcony one evening, he had reservations. "I am dreadfully disappointed at the spirit here," he wrote to one of his four daughters. Later Lee observed, "Our people here have . . . endeavored to prove they ought to do nothing. This is not the way to accomplish our independence."

Coastal defenses were too dispersed, Lee saw instantly. He began constricting and strengthening the lines. This meant major construction works by males of all classes. Lee showed a courteous imperviousness to the outrage of citizen-soldiers whose idea of a chivalric war he offended. In a November 22 letter to his daughters, he said with a tinge of sarcasm: "I hope the enemy will be polite enough to wait for us" to get ready.

Lion of the Valley

Gen. Stonewall Jackson in Winchester, Virginia,
November 6, 1861

The Richmond *Daily Dispatch* said of
Jackson's new assignment: "He will prove
himself an instance of the right man in the right
place." Yet as Jackson surveyed his domain, he
felt challenge rather than optimism.

　　He found himself a commander without a
command—a general in charge of a defenseless
district. Waiting for him at Winchester in
December were three militia brigades with
a total of 1,500 men. About 300 were armed
with flintlock muskets; the remainder had no
arms. The ranks had so thinned from members
enlisting in the army that colonels led company-
size units. All lacked discipline and experience.
In addition, 10,000 Federal troops were in
positions to the north and west of Winchester.

　　Jackson got back the Stonewall Brigade to
use as a core for buildup of trained soldiers. In
the months ahead he would mold a Confederate
force small in number but mobile in movement.
Winchester attorney Robert Conrad wrote a
soldier-son that Jackson's presence "has had
great effect upon the spirits of our citizens . . .
and inspired confidence in our safety."

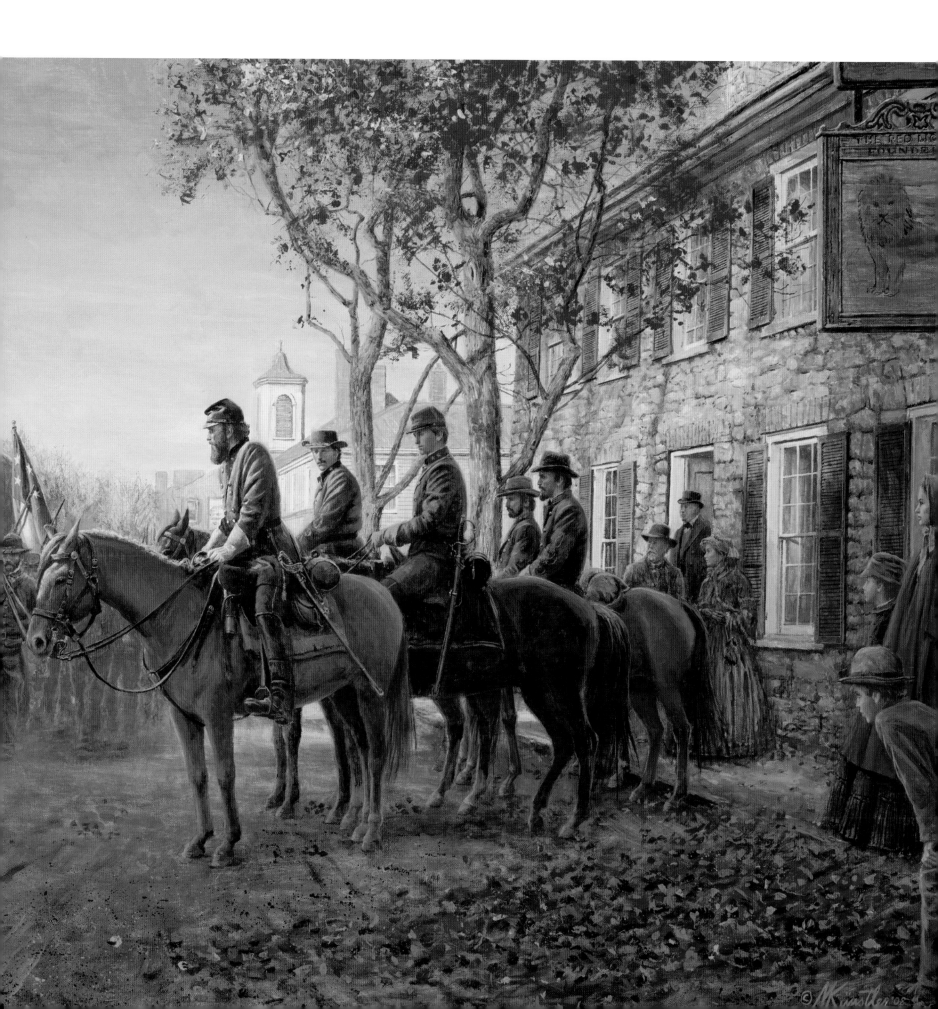

Guns of Autumn

Gen. Robert E. Lee in Charleston, South Carolina, December 15, 1861

Moving heavy coastal guns past the Exchange Building, the city's post office, was a novel sight for Charlestonians. So was the appearance of Lee. Well-known poet and literary critic Paul Hamilton Hayne recorded his first impression: "In the midst of the group, topping the tallest by half a head was, perhaps, the most striking figure we had ever encountered . . . erect as a poplar, yet lithe and graceful, with broad shoulders well thrown back . . . clear, deep, thoughtful eyes, and the quiet dauntless step of one every inch the gentleman and soldier."

President Davis summoned Lee back to Richmond early in March 1862. His accomplishments along the Atlantic coast remained unknown to the general populace. However, one authority wrote, "so impregnable was the defensive system he constructed in three months that neither Charleston nor Savannah, surviving constant and heavy bombardment, was taken from the sea or by flanking amphibious operations."

Before the Battle

Stonewall Jackson and Staff

Good staff work was essential for success in the large and highly personal Civil War. "Stonewall" Jackson is credited with having one of the best groups of assistants in either army. These men made up the core of his inner circle. In the painting, Jackson stands at far right.

In the back row, from left to right, are:

HUNTER MCGUIRE, medical director: one of the most promising surgeons in Virginia at the outbreak of the war; later president of the American Medical Association.

JEDEDIAH HOTCHKISS, mapmaker: he held no military rank but produced the finest maps of the Civil War.

ALEXANDER S. PENDLETON, chief of staff: young and highly attentive. To any small question asked, Jackson would reply: "Ask Sandie Pendleton. If he does not know, no one does."

JAMES POWER SMITH, aide: a theological student, he and Jackson enjoyed an almost father-son relationship.

HENRY KYD DOUGLAS, aide: not as accomplished as his memoirs imply, but he served and observed Jackson well.

JOHN A. HARMAN, quartermaster: big-bodied, gruff, possessed of such a mastery of profanity—he could curse so loudly, so passionately, and so threateningly—that he could single-handedly unsnarl the most hopelessly stuck wagon train, scaring man and beast alike into extraordinary efforts.

In the left foreground:

WELLS J. HAWKS, commissary of subsistence: prominent businessman and former state legislator, with good connections to sources of supplies.

Stonewall Jackson and Staff

Until We Meet Again

Jackson's Headquarters, Winchester, Virginia, December, 1861 *(below)*

A Fleeting Moment

Winchester, Virginia, February 1, 1862 *(opposite)*

Anna Morrison became the greatest joy in Jackson's life. She was the daughter of a Presbyterian minister who became the first president of Davidson College in North Carolina. In young adulthood, Anna made occasional visits to a sister in Lexington, Virginia. There she met Prof. Thomas Jackson of the Virginia Military Institute.

His first wife had died in 1854 in childbirth. Three years later, despite the fact that Jackson was seven and a half years older, Anna married the lonely widower. She brought much to the union. Outgoing and sociable, she gently pulled her husband from his shell of shyness. Anna also shared ardently Jackson's faith in the presence and power of God.

During the Civil War, the couple was together on four occasions. The longest tenure came in the winter of 1861–62, when they lived with Rev. James Graham's family a few doors from Jackson's headquarters in Winchester. Jackson attended studiously to his military duties, but the stern general was a loving husband whenever he was with his *esposita* (the affectionate word he used for Anna). His wife was privy to the gentleness that lay behind the unbending countenance. "He was the most tender, affectionate and demonstrative man at home that I ever saw," she recalled. "His heart was as soft as a woman's. He was full of love and tenderness."

To Jackson, Anna was "a gift from our Heavenly Father." He addressed one of his first war letters to "my darling pet" and confessed: "I would very much like to see my sweet little face, but my darling had better remain at her own home, as much continuance here is very uncertain."

Their three months together at Winchester was an idyllic time. It ended with the coming of spring and renewal of military movements. Anna was pregnant when she returned to her parental home. She would not see her husband again for thirteen months.

"He was the most tender, affectionate and demonstrative

man at home that I ever saw."

—Anna Jackson

CHAPTER THREE

IN SEARCH OF VICTORY

January 1862—June 1863

I N 1862, TIDAL WAVES OF BATTLE SWEPT across the width of America, splashing horror and blood in every corner of the once-united nation. Fighting escalated; combat and suffering exceeded human imagination; heartbreak became a common emotion.

Armies traditionally did not campaign in the cold months, but two of the Civil War's most famous generals made exceptions to the rule in the war's first winter.

Since November 1861, protection of Virginia's Shenandoah Valley consisted of 3,000 veterans, recruits, and militia under the command of Manassas hero "Stonewall" Jackson. He was a restless man who always considered offense the best weapon to use for defense. The indefatigable general quickly created an army through enlistments, transfer of units from outlying areas, and the addition of two veteran brigades—including his own Stonewall Brigade. For a time, his force numbered 11,000 troops. On New Year's Day 1862, Jackson departed Winchester with his command. His aim was to clear Federal units from nearby railroad stations and river crossings twenty-five miles to the northwest in Romney (in present-day West Virginia).

Balmy weather changed overnight to freezing temperatures and wind-driven snow. Jackson was imperturbable to the elements. The Romney Campaign lasted three weeks and only momentarily achieved its objectives. Yet it demonstrated Jackson's ever-present eagerness to strike the enemy at any time and under any circumstances.

Two weeks later, across the Appalachian Mountain barrier in Tennessee, another field commander gained two easy victories for the North.

Control of the major rivers was the key to success there. In early September 1861, Confederates had broken Kentucky's neutrality and seized the small town of Columbus, which became a commanding fortress overlooking the upper Mississippi River. The North responded with a "river war" of its own. A force under a plain, little-known general from Illinois, Ulysses S. Grant, marched forty miles upriver and occupied Paducah. There both the Tennessee and Cumberland rivers emptied into the Ohio.

Opposing Grant was Confederate general Albert Sidney Johnston, a soldier with thirty years' experience and regarded by many as the South's ablest commander. Johnston lacked both manpower and supplies to maintain a four-hundred-mile defensive line stretching from Cumberland Gap to the Mississippi River. Seeing these weaknesses, Grant soon began a campaign unique in two ways. Not only was it a wintertime offensive; it was one incorporating both an army and a navy of new ironclad gunboats.

On February 4, 1862, the Union force started up the Tennessee River, which had its headwaters in northern Alabama. A lone Confederate defense, Fort Henry, stood on low ground and was half-flooded when Federals arrived. The garrison surrendered on February 6 after heavy naval fire. Grant then turned east to Fort Donelson, twelve miles away. It was the South's principal defense on the Cumberland River, which led to Nashville, Tennessee's state capital and a major supply center in the West.

Snow fell, and the temperature dropped into the teens. Confederates inside Fort Donelson waged a good fight against first gunboats and then infantry. Yet owing to the ineptitude of the fort's commanders, Donelson became a death trap. Grant's demand for "immediate and unconditional surrender" resulted in close to 15,000 Confederate prisoners and brought the Union general a nickname, "Unconditional Surrender" Grant. Half of Tennessee and its two principal rivers were now in Federal hands.

Sidney Johnston fell back beyond the loop of the Tennessee River to the rail junction of Corinth, Mississippi. In the face of bad weather and several epidemics of sickness, he rebuilt a larger army and then launched a surprise attack. At dawn on April 6, Johnston's men assailed the napping Union army at Shiloh. Johnston was killed in the first day's action. Confederates were slowly driven back in defeat the following day.

Over 100,000 men were engaged in combat at Shiloh. One of every four was killed, wounded, or captured. The 23,000 casualties at this early point in the Civil War proved conclusively that the American volunteer, from both North and South, could fight—and fight bravely.

New Orleans, the South's largest city, surrendered to Union naval forces late in April. "The country is shrouded in gloom," Judith McGuire of Richmond wrote in her journal. "Oh, it is so hard seeing the enemy making such inroads into the heart of our country."

Meanwhile, for months on the Virginia front, Gen. McClellan perfected, polished, and paraded his Army of the Potomac in the fields around Washington. Weather was favorable, roads were good, the army was in excellent spirits. Lincoln urged McClellan to attack the Confederate army wintering just across the Potomac. The ever-cautious McClellan balked: he considered maneuver, not battle, the key to victory. Hence, while Lincoln wanted the massive Union army to engage in a head-on checkers game with Gen. Joseph E. Johnston's forces, McClellan preferred to play a chess game and checkmate his opponent by capturing Richmond. Lincoln grudgingly acquiesced to McClellan's wishes in order to get some sort of action from the North's principal army.

Throughout March and April, McClellan used 389 transport vessels to transfer 120,000 soldiers, 15,000 animals, 1,200 supply wagons, and hundreds of tons of equipment "secretly" down the Potomac River and Chesapeake Bay to the vicinity of Yorktown. From there the Union army would march unmolested up the peninsula formed by the York and James rivers. Richmond would be seized and the Civil War would end.

Nothing went right for McClellan from the start.

When Virginians captured the Norfolk navy yard in April 1861, they raised the USS *Merrimack*, encased it in armor, renamed it the CSS *Virginia*, and sent it to clear the Norfolk harbor of Union blockaders. The great ironclad sank two Federal wooden ships before the North responded with its own ironclad. The USS *Monitor* was a revolutionary-looking vessel likened to "a tin can on a shingle." *Monitor* and *Virginia* spent several hours on March 9, 1862, in a close-fought duel that ended in a draw. The presence of the *Virginia* on his flank unnerved McClellan.

Worse, Joseph Johnston had abandoned the northern Virginia region and was waiting for the Union army when it disembarked at Yorktown. However, with only 40,000 Confederates at hand, Johnston had no choice but to give ground slowly in the face of McClellan's advance. Mother Nature proved an ally to the Confederates, slowing down the massive Union army. Rain fell throughout the month of May and turned the countryside into an ocean of mud. Federal soldiers struggled against the elements as well as McClellan's timidity.

"Victory has no charm for me."

—Gen. George B. McClellan

By the end of May, McClellan had inched to within nine miles of Richmond. Suddenly Johnston struck an isolated flank of McClellan's army at the hamlet of Seven Pines. Johnston fell seriously wounded during two days of assaults that, while accomplishing little tactically, brought McClellan's offensive to a halt. "Victory has no charm for me," McClellan wrote after seeing "mangled corpses" strewn on the battlefield.

Further woes came to the Union general from 175 miles to the west. The fertile Shenandoah Valley was both the "Breadbasket of the Confederacy" and a geographical avenue into the heart of the North. Defending it at the beginning of spring was Stonewall Jackson.

Jackson had about 3,400 troops in the valley. Outnumbered almost three to one, he nevertheless attacked his opponent on March 23 at Kernstown. This engagement alarmed Union officials fearful for the safety of Washington, especially after reinforcements tripled the size of Jackson's force. One of the war's most brilliant campaigns followed. In two months, Jackson's soldiers marched 670 miles, fought a half dozen engagements, defeated three separate Federal hosts, and cleared the valley of all Union threats. "We have drawn the Yankees from the Valley," Pvt. Charles Trueheart of the Rockbridge Artillery wrote his brother. "God has seen fit to very greatly bless our arms in this district."

Robert E. Lee also played a major role in the Confederate turnabout.

After Johnston's wounding, President Jefferson Davis named Lee to command of the Army of Northern Virginia. Lee had never led troops in the field, but he would now demonstrate an amazing audacity. While McClellan should have been thinking of action but did not, Lee should have been thinking of defense but did not. The new Southern commander made preparations to do exactly what Sidney Johnston had done at Shiloh—strike the unsuspecting invader.

Starting on June 26, 1862, with Jackson's force en route from the valley, Lee assailed McClellan's right flank. The Seven Days Campaign followed. At Mechanicsville, Gaines' Mill (where Jackson joined Lee on the twenty-seventh),

Savage Station, Glendale, and Malvern Hill, the Army of Northern Virginia hammered McClellan's army. The Union commander avoided destruction by retreating to the James River and the protection of naval big guns.

Casualties were appalling for Americans unfamiliar with war. Northern losses that week were 16,500 soldiers. Few Union officers agreed with McClellan's retreat across the peninsula. Gen. Darius Couch wrote: "The soldiers who had fought so magnificently for the last week, marching by night and fighting by day, were now a mob."

Lee suffered 20,600 casualties, roughly a fourth of his command. Yet for the moment, Lee had saved Richmond.

Federal pressure on Virginia quickly came from another quarter. Bombastic Gen. John Pope put together a new army of some 77,000 troops and began moving through the Virginia piedmont. His goal was to capture the central Virginia rail junction at Gordonsville and proceed southeast to Richmond's back door.

The outnumbered Lee again took the initiative. Convinced that McClellan had no intention of resuming his offensive, Lee dispatched Jackson to confront Pope. Jackson's men stopped Pope's advance in a sharp August 9 fight at Cedar Mountain, south of Culpeper. This was the hottest battle day of the war. It was 98 degrees in midafternoon.

Two weeks later, McClellan having abandoned the peninsula, Lee joined Jackson. The commanding general devised quick and bold strategy. Jackson's half of the army would swing widely around the Union army and get in Pope's rear. When Pope naturally turned and started after Jackson, Lee would move on Pope from the opposite direction—the two halves closing in like a vise. The risks involved were large: Lee was dividing his force in the face of a numerically superior force. The two wings would be out of touch for the better part of two days. In an incredible march of fifty-six miles, Jackson and his "foot cavalry" cut the major railroad in the area and destroyed Pope's supply base at Manassas Junction.

An angry Pope started after Jackson. Lee started after Pope. The elements came together August 28–30 in heavy fighting at Second Manassas. Pope's men were driven from the field in a Southern victory as conclusive as First Manassas had been.

Virginia was momentarily free of Federal armies. In ninety days Lee had changed the war in the East from a contest for Richmond

There Were Never Such Men,
Gen. Lee and His Staff

to a threat against Washington. Lee considered the Federal capital too fortified to attack. On the other hand, a campaign into the North, with a victory on Union soil, might provoke overwhelming cries for peace from Northern citizens. Such a success could also bring the foreign recognition from European governments that would enhance the South's hope for independence.

Lee crossed the Potomac early in September. A defiant Union garrison at Harpers Ferry compelled Lee to split his forces into three separate wings. By accident, a copy of Lee's marching orders fell into the possession of the carefully trailing McClellan. The Union general suddenly knew not only Lee's positions but also his intentions.

The sixteen hours that McClellan spent digesting the information gave Lee just enough time to concentrate his forces along Antietam Creek at Sharpsburg, Maryland. Wednesday, September 17, became the bloodiest one-day battle in American history. Rather than hurl his vastly superior numbers at Lee's thin, improvised line, McClellan attacked in stages from one end of the field to the other. First were assaults against Jackson, manning Lee's left. Then came strikes against a sunken road that was the center of the Confederate line. Thirteen hours of combat ended with the fighting on Lee's right at Burnside Bridge.

Confederates gave ground but never retreated. When McClellan did not renew the offensive the following day, Lee's battered army returned to Virginia.

Over 23,300 men were killed, wounded, or captured in the fighting at Antietam. Had all of those casualties been laid shoulder to shoulder, the line would have extended four and a half miles.

Antietam was not a clear-cut Northern victory, but President Lincoln saw it as sufficient grounds for issuing a preliminary Emancipation Proclamation, on September 22. Slaves in states or part of states still in rebellion on January 1, 1863, were declared to be "then, thenceforward, and forever free." This announcement created a national storm of controversy. Future events would determine its fate.

In the West that autumn, another Confederate offense failed. Gen. Braxton Bragg could fashion an army well; he lacked the personality to lead it successfully. As Lee's troops waded across the Potomac into Maryland, Bragg's Army of Tennessee swung into Kentucky in two wings that never quite came together. The Southern invasion ran aground October 8 at Perryville, where opposing armies collided in search of springs of badly needed water.

Bragg abandoned the offensive and retired all the way to Murfreesboro, Tennessee. There, beginning December 31 and lasting three days, Union and Confederate forces waged a confused, bloody contest along Stones River. Bragg again retreated from the field. The Army of Tennessee saw no other action for the next six months.

One battle remained to be fought that year, in Virginia. It was Lee's most lopsided triumph.

Following the November off-year elections in the North, and with Republicans still firmly in political control, Lincoln's long patience with McClellan faded. He sent the general into retirement. McClellan's successor was the unassuming and likable Ambrose E. Burnside.

Burnside stole a march on Lee and shifted his forces to the Rappahannock River, opposite Fredericksburg. His plan was to drive between Lee's army and Richmond, from which position he could either fight Lee on good ground or march to the Confederate capital.

Burnside's advance troops reached Falmouth, near Fredericksburg, on November 17 as planned, but everything depended on the appearance of several dozen clumsy wooden scows that the army used for pontoon bridges. They were nowhere in sight. No pontoons, no bridges; no bridges, no crossing of the Rappahannock.

Seeing nothing else to do, Burnside sat quietly and waited. The boats began to arrive a week later, and Burnside waited two more weeks before making a move. By then, Lee had 72,500 veterans packed in earthworks on the hills behind Fredericksburg. The line was unbreakable. Burnside spent all day of December 13 trying to prove otherwise.

"Old Jack's" New Uniform (study)
High Command at Fredericksburg, December 13, 1862

"It is well that **war is so terrible**; else we should grow too fond of it."

—Gen. Robert E. Lee

It was a sad battle in that common heroism and sacrifice were so enormously displayed and so pitifully wasted. Fourteen times Federals made head-on attacks against Lee's position. Fourteen times the columns were shot to pieces. At one point, Lee looked out at the slaughter and commented: "It is well that war is so terrible; else we should grow too fond of it."

The Army of the Potomac suffered over 12,000 casualties and a good deal of its morale. Lee's losses were half that number.

A month later, Burnside tried to move upstream, cross the Rappahannock, and get beyond Lee's flank. Barely had the march begun when three days of sleet and snow turned the country into depthless, icy mud. The army had no choice but to abandon the "Mud March" and struggle back to Fredericksburg, thoroughly dispirited.

Meanwhile, the Emancipation Proclamation became law on January 1, 1863. Although it announced freedom only for those slaves inside the Confederacy, it was an irrevocable, first step in making human freedom and preservation of the Union twin goals of the Northern war effort. Some 180,000 ex-slaves ultimately became Federal soldiers. They earned their freedom fighting for it amid crass discrimination.

In the Western theater, following the Union victory at Stones River, Grant shifted attention to America's largest river. He began tightening the noose around the last Confederate stronghold on the Mississippi: Vicksburg.

War's heavy hand pressed down hard throughout the war's second winter. Several months earlier, an Albany, New York, newspaper had made a dark prediction: "We have learned that the contest between us and the Confederates is reduced to a question of pure brute force. . . . that there is no middle ground—no half-way house—between absolute triumph and absolute vassalage."

Feelings became deeper and more personal. Even enemy soldiers began to find that emotions other than duty might bring small relief. Some units strengthened their reputation through endurance. Others knew a moment of fame. On the Southern home front, by and large, an attitude of acceptance of what one could not change became the way of life. Months earlier, the matronly Judith McGuire noted: "Our people continue to make every effort to repel the foe, who, like the locusts of Egypt, overrun our land."

Lee's forces huddled during the cold months in a twenty-five-mile line along the Rappahannock. Exposure to the elements, lack of supplies, and loneliness were constant companions among most Southern troops. Lee and Jackson were the bonds that held the army intact.

Even those two generals had low moments that winter. Late in the season, Lee suffered a heart attack from which he never fully recovered. Jackson lost a dear friend, a young child who had become like a daughter. Fortunately, a visit from his wife and the five-month-old daughter he now saw for the first time helped overcome his grief.

While Confederates struggled through the winter, Lincoln replaced Burnside with the pompous and aggressive Joseph Hooker. Having openly coveted the job, Hooker

"We have learned that the contest between us and the Confederates is reduced to a question of pure brute force. . . . that there is no middle ground—no half-way house—between absolute triumph and absolute vassalage."

—*Albany Evening Journal,* August 9, 1862

first restored morale with back pay, furloughs, corps badges, and reorganization. The change of attitude inside the ranks steadily rose. One soldier remarked that Hooker proved "a veritable Santa Claus to the army."

The new Union commander then devised a brilliant strategy for the spring. He left a third of his army to hold Lee's attention at Fredericksburg. The remainder Hooker took on a long movement up and across the Rappahannock and Rapidan rivers in order to get around Lee's unprotected flank and rear. That would squeeze Lee between two Federal wings. His alternatives would be to retreat or to fight Hooker on grounds of the Union general's choosing.

Two things then went wrong for the Federals. Hooker inexplicably halted his force six miles from open country inside a thick, dark, and confused timberland known as the Wilderness. Lee, in the most daring move of his entire career, split his little army into three pieces and launched an attack of his own on May 2.

Jackson led his men on another flank march, this one through stifling heat. Fighting began late in the day in the Wilderness and raged there, at Fredericksburg, and around Salem Church between Fredericksburg and Chancellorsville. The strangely passive Hooker held 30,000 men out of action. Finally, with Lee's army fighting on two fronts, Hooker had an opportunity to redeem the whole situation. Instead, he reportedly said "I just lost faith in Joe Hooker" and retreated across the Rappahannock.

The battle of Chancellorsville went on until May 6. In the end, Hooker suffered 17,000 casualties and personal humiliation. Lee lost a fourth of his army, including his ablest lieutenant, Stonewall Jackson.

Spring became summer, and the two armies were back on opposite sides of the Rappahannock where they had been when the year began. Yet Confederate forces sensed an air of pending activity. Gen. Dorsey Pender wrote his wife: "All feel that something is brewing and that Gen. Lee is not going to wait all the time for them to come to him."

With the Union grip slowly tightening in both East and West, Lee reasoned that if the Confederates could win

a spectacular victory on Northern soil, the Union government might see the futility of the war and allow the South to have its independence. In June, with the irreplaceable Jackson, much of the officer corps, and thousands of his veterans missing from death or wounds, Lee resolved to strike northward again.

> "All feel that something is brewing and that Gen. **Lee is not going to wait** all the time for them to come to him."
>
> —Gen. Dorsey Pender

The Winds of Winter

Jackson's Romney Campaign, Virginia, January 1862

Jackson's inspiring leadership could not prevent the exposure, sickness, and demoralization experienced by the troops during the Romney campaign. The weather was awful. Freezing winds chilled the men to the bone as they struggled at times through inches of snow. Supply wagons were unable to keep pace. Many nights the soldiers bivouacked in the open without food or adequate clothing. When the temperature rose, the countryside became a sea of mud.

The movement was reminiscent of Napoleon crossing the Alps in May 1800. Virginia's Kyd Douglas noted: "The road was almost an uninterrupted sheet of ice. . . . By moonlight the beards of the men, matted with ice and glistening like crystals, presented a very peculiar but ludicrous appearance. I have not been able to find a man in the 2nd Reg. who did not fall down at least twice."

Young Lt. James Langhorne of Jackson's Headquarters Guard confessed in a letter: "Ma, the romance of the thing is entirely worn off, not only with myself but with the whole army."

Jackson was a stern taskmaster indeed.

After the Snow

Winchester, Virginia, January 6, 1862

Winchester, Virginia, was the northern doorway to the Shenandoah Valley. Seven roads (two macadamized) radiated from the town and made it a leading market center for that region. One of the North's major railroads, the Baltimore & Ohio, lay twenty miles to the north.

The city of 4,000 inhabitants became innocent bystanders to war in full force, Cornelia McDonald remembered: "Those days of preparation for battle were holiday days compared with what came after. We, the ladies, worked increasingly making lint, rolling bandages . . . making jackets and trousers. . . . Even tents were made by fingers that had scarcely ever used a needle before."

Three major battles and more than fifty minor engagements took place for control of Winchester. The town changed hands more than seventy times in the four years of war. Lt. Col. Arthur Fremantle, a visiting British officer, observed in 1863: "The unfortunate town of Winchester seems to have been made a regular shuttlecock of by the contending armies."

Rebel Sons of Erin

Fort Donelson Campaign, Tennessee, February 13, 1862

Some 185,000 Irish immigrants served in the Civil War: about 145,000 fought for the Union army, and 40,000 for the Confederate. Immensely proud people, they tended to organize into all-Irish units. One such regiment was the 10th Tennessee, dubbed the "Rebel Sons of Erin."

Their colonel was Randal McGavock, a Harvard law graduate, world traveler, and former Nashville mayor. McGavock furnished his 720 men with special uniforms and their own enormous regimental flag. Yet the recruits departed for war with government-issue flintlock muskets that were relics from the War of 1812.

On February 13, 1862, the Irishmen, mostly inexperienced recruits, were manning an advanced position at Fort Donelson. Hastily constructed parapets consisted of logs and brush covered with dirt. Subfreezing temperature and several inches of snow on the ground added to the troops' discomfort.

Suddenly three Illinois regiments attacked them. McGavock wrote in his journal: "My Reg. behaved nobly and was as much as I could do to keep them in the pits, they were so anxious to get out and charge them. The fight lasted fifteen or twenty minutes but was terrible while it lasted."

This was the only time in the war when the 10th Tennessee as a whole participated in a battle. McGavock was killed in a May 1863 engagement at Raymond, Mississippi.

The Ghost Column

Col. Nathan Bedford Forrest, Fort Donelson, February 16, 1862

Nathan Bedford Forrest was one of the most unusual cavalry officers in the Civil War. A former Memphis slave trader without social status or military background, he had an intuitive sense for battle and a grinding, man-killing nature in combat. "Forrest never did anything as anyone else would have done or even thought of doing in regards to a fight," trooper William Witherspoon stated.

At Fort Donelson, Forrest was in charge of a detachment of cavalry. When the besieged garrison commanders decided to lay down their arms, the hard, rough-hewn Forrest had no intention of giving up the fight. "Boys!" he shouted to his men. "These people are talking about surrendering. I am going out of this place before they do or bust hell wide open!" At 4 a.m. on February 17, Forrest roused 500 shivering horsemen and 100 infantrymen. Slowly they moved in column through the cold darkness. For thirty hours, through snow and frigid winds, the column wound its way 110 miles to safety.

"Boys! These **people are talking about surrendering.** I am going out of this place before they do or **bust hell wide open!**"

—Col. Nathan Bedford Forrest

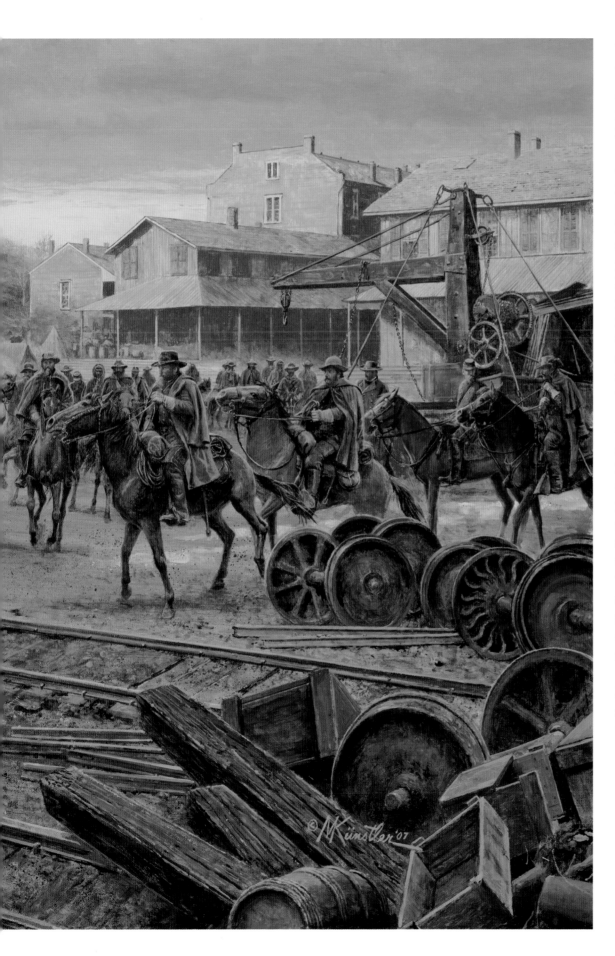

Order Out of Chaos

Col. Nathan Bedford Forrest, Nashville, Tennessee, February 22, 1862

On reaching their goal, Nashville, Forrest and his men found not welcome but chaos. Reports of Fort Donelson's fall and rumors of a rapidly approaching Union army had created pandemonium. Nashville editor John McKee wrote: "The town was in a perfect tumult—a furor that lashed into a phrenzy those who were regarded perfect models of the calm and passionless— and the wave [spread] with fearful rapidity." Local law enforcement was nonexistent.

Forrest quickly seized control of warehouses being looted. His men attacked mobs with flashing swords, loud profanity, and a fire engine loaded with icy water from the Cumberland River. Forrest then impressed every available vehicle and transferred foodstuffs, ammunition, and clothing to a railroad line. His men even brought off rifling machinery from a local foundry. Forrest destroyed the remaining goods and evacuated the city just as Union soldiers reached the outskirts.

The groggy and half-empty Nashville was the first state capital to fall into Federal control, but Forrest would appear again—and often.

Confederate Winter

Gen. Richard Taylor
at Swift Run Gap, Virginia,
March 1862

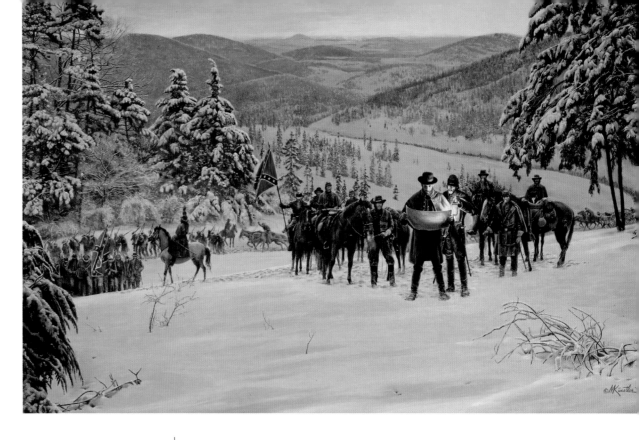

Gen. Richard Taylor's brigade of Louisianans had never encountered a Virginia spring "coming in with its accustomed severity," as he later wrote in his memoir. The 800 men from the lower Mississippi region got a painful awakening in March 1862, when they received orders to cross the Blue Ridge Mountains and join Stonewall Jackson's command in the Shenandoah Valley. Each man was to carry only the barest necessities.

A steady, soaking downpour began with the march. Rain turned to sleet, then to snow. For ten days, men struggled up and through the mountains. The column became subdued as soldiers fought cold and deep snow. "We have nothing," one Louisianan grumbled, "but march, march, and halt and sleep in wet blankets."

The men marched through the mountain pass with lightning and thunder filling the sky. Then, as suddenly as it began, the storm passed. Brilliant sunlight shone as the soldiers moved down into the valley. Reflecting later on the ordeal, a member of the Louisiana Tigers confessed to his wife: "I thought that I knowed something a bout Soldiering, but I find that I had never Soldiered it this way."

USS Monitor vs. CSS Virginia

Hampton Roads, Virginia, March 9, 1862

Few naval duels have been more revolutionary than the action at Hampton Roads, Virginia, on March 9, 1862.

When Virginia forces captured the abandoned navy yards at Norfolk in April 1861, they found the partially scuttled steam frigate USS *Merrimack*. Resourceful Southerners proceeded to convert the vessel into a fighting ship unprecedented in history. The superstructure had a slanting side of oak two feet thick, on which was laid a four-inch coating of iron. Ports existed for ten guns. To one observer, the CSS *Virginia* was "a barn gone adrift and submerged to the eaves."

While the *Virginia* was under construction, the Union navy was hard at work on its own ironclad. The USS *Monitor* resembled "a tin can on a shingle"—flat hull barely visible above water, with a revolving turret mounting two eleven-inch guns. Smaller than the *Virginia*, the *Monitor* was more maneuverable.

On March 8, in the Norfolk harbor, the *Virginia* destroyed two wooden warships and ran three other vessels aground. The next day, the *Monitor* appeared. The two ironclads spent almost four hours in a close-range fight that did no serious damage to either. (Since warships had never worn armor, no armor-piercing shells had been produced.)

Union naval captain Gershom Van Brunt stated in wonder:

"Never before was anything like it dreamed of by the greatest enthusiast in maritime warfare." By the end of that day, every wooden navy in the world was obsolete.

Rush's Lancers

Peninsula Campaign, Camp Meigs, Philadelphia, spring 1862 *(opposite, bottom)*

Patriotic fervor in the first months of the Civil War was never more in evidence than with Rush's Lancers. Composed in the main of Philadelphia's raw youth, the recruits knew nothing about riding and caring for horses. Their determined leader was a Pennsylvania aristocrat, Richard Rush, a West Point graduate whose grandfather had signed the Declaration of Independence.

It was Gen. George McClellan who, in late summer of 1861, suggested that Rush's unit (officially the 6th Pennsylvania Cavalry Regiment) arm itself with lances. Napoleon had made good use of the weapons a half-century earlier when war was less sophisticated. Rush's young troopers did not take kindly to the nine-foot wooden lance with an eleven-inch steel blade and red banner on the end. One Lancer considered the weapon "a decided nuisance in a wooded country." Lavish uniforms also made the regiment conspicuous—to friend and foe alike.

Fortunately, the regiment never saw action with their vintage lances. When the Pennsylvanians arrived on the Virginia peninsula in the spring of 1862, cavalry commander George Stoneman told Rush to throw away "them Damn poles" and arm themselves with conventional weapons. That was the end of lances in the Civil War.

The Fight at Fallen Timbers

Forrest and Morgan at Shiloh, Tennessee, April 8, 1862

A month after Hampton Roads, in Tennessee, Confederates abandoned the Shiloh battlefield after two days of fiery combat and retreated southward in the rain. Gen. William Tecumseh Sherman's weary Federals started a half-hearted pursuit. On April 8, on a patch of ground littered with trees from a prewar logging camp (and appropriately named Fallen Timbers), Union infantry received some unexpected visitors.

Some 350 Southern cavalry, Sherman reported, "came down boldly at a charge, led by General Forrest in person, breaking through our line of skirmishers; when the regiment of infantry, without cause, broke, threw away their muskets and fled."

An overexuberant Forrest galloped ahead of his men and quickly found himself surrounded by Union soldiers yelling "Shoot him! Kill him! Stick him!" The scowling Forrest fired his revolver as he slashed left and right with his saber. A Union bullet pierced his left side; his horse received mortal wounds. Forrest broke clear of the Federal pack, grabbed an unsuspecting soldier, and pulled him onto the horse behind him. The colonel used the man as a shield until he reached his waiting troops. Forrest casually dropped the man to the ground as his horse collapsed in death.

Duty, Honor, and Tears

Long Branch, Millwood, Virginia, May 24, 1862

As Clarke County's representative to the Virginia secession convention, Hugh Mortimer Nelson did not want disunion or war. He was content to live in peace at Long Branch, one of the most beautiful estates in the foothills of the Blue Ridge Mountains. Friends knew Nelson as "a man of wondrous charm of manner and bearing." He and his wife had two children. They were an adoring family.

War called, however, and Nelson followed his duty to Virginia.

He served as a captain of cavalry until his promotion to major and assignment to the staff of Gen. Richard S. Ewell. A fellow officer called Nelson "as fine, brave an old fellow as ever lived."

On May 23, 1862, Ewell's division was passing through Clarke County with Stonewall Jackson's forces. Nelson received permission for an overnight visit home. It was a quick reunion and an even more emotional farewell. Two and a half months later, Nelson died of typhoid fever.

Gen. Thomas "Stonewall" Jackson *(above)* • Especially for You *(right)*

Winchester, Virginia, May 25, 1862

No army of liberation had ever met deeper gratefulness.

In midmorning, May 25, Jackson's forces broke the Union lines south of Winchester. Federals bolted through town and toward the Potomac like "a mass of disorganized fugitives," Jackson reported. His Confederates then marched victoriously through downtown Winchester.

"I never saw such a demonstration," Capt. James Edmondson of the 27th Virginia declared. "Every window was crowded and every door was filled with them and all . . . waving handkerchiefs and flags and others were engaged in supplying the soldiers as they passed with food and water."

Charles Trueheart of the Rockbridge Artillery was more impressed. "To the day of my death, I shall never forget the scene that greeted our delighted eyes. . . . On all sides—from windows, on the side walks, and porches were throngs of the fair young ladies, and hospitable matrons, old men and children, hurrahing and shouting for joy . . . at our arrival, and their being rid of the detested Yankee rule."

Jackson's face was "alight with the glow of his triumphant pursuit," a teenager remarked. Jackson himself later wrote his wife with unusual excitement: "The people seemed nearly frantic with joy; indeed it would be almost impossible to describe their manifestations of rejoicing and gratitude. Our entrance into Winchester was one of the most stirring scenes of my life."

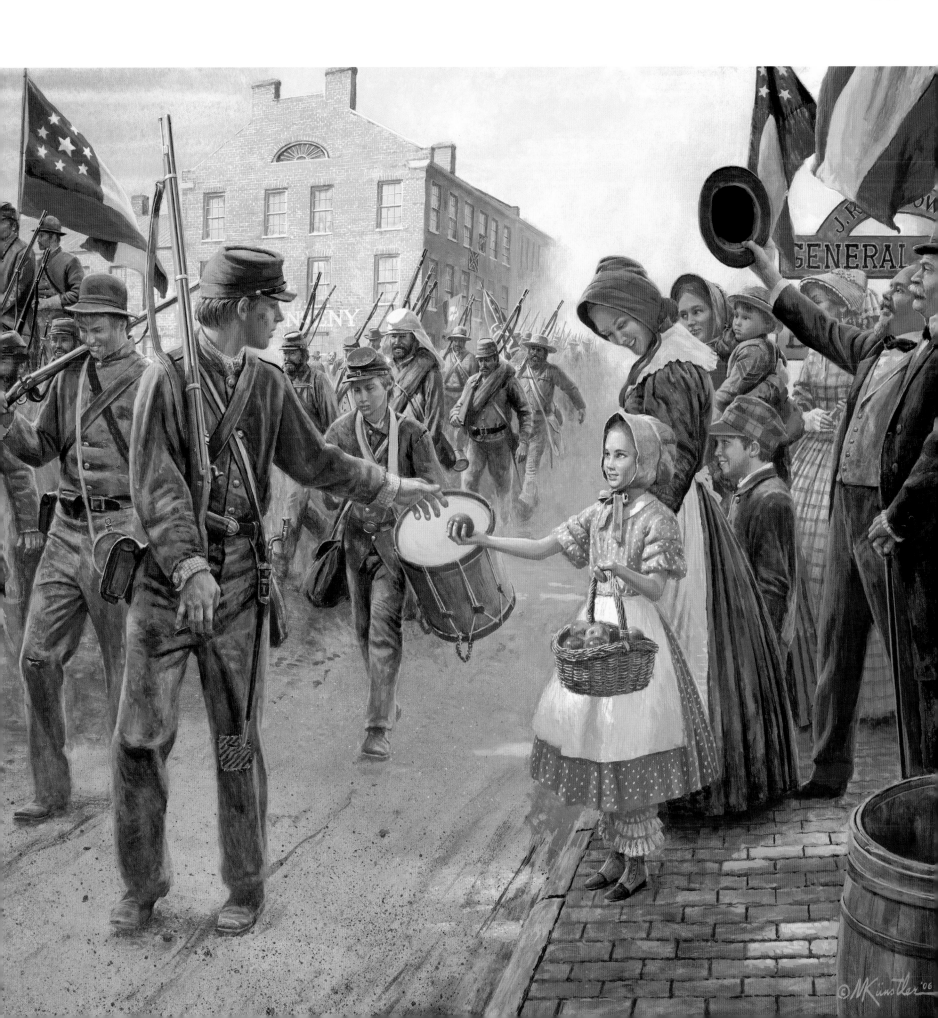

Lee Takes Command

Pres. Davis and Gen. Lee, May 31, 1862 *(below)*

The May 31 battle at Seven Pines was intense and frightfully mismanaged. Confederates gained little as casualties soared. President Davis and Gen. Lee, both on the field, watched helplessly. Near nightfall, Gen. Joseph Johnston fell, seriously wounded. It was a critical hour for the Confederacy, and the next day might be even worse.

Davis and Lee started back to Richmond. At the edge of the battlefield, Davis turned in the saddle. "General Lee," he said, "I shall assign you to command of this army. Make your preparations as quickly as you can. I will issue the necessary order when we get to Richmond."

Now Lee would do what he had never done in thirty-seven years as a soldier: lead troops in combat. Col. Robert H. Gray of the 22nd North Carolina was unimpressed by Lee's appointment: "He makes no show or parade and rides about from one point to another as quietly as a farmer would ride over his farm." Yet Joseph Ives of Lee's staff thought otherwise. "Lee is audacity personified," Ives stated. Henceforth, Lee and the Army of Northern Virginia would be one.

Jackson's "Foot Cavalry"

Old Mill, Strasburg, Virginia, June 1, 1862 *(opposite)*

They were farmers, students, and shopkeepers who lived in the valley and along the hills of the west side of the Blue Ridge Mountains. At the call to arms, they had enlisted in the 2nd, 4th, 5th, 27th, and 33rd Virginia Infantry Regiments. A valiant stand at the opening battle of the war earned them the name "Stonewall Brigade," and the title became a lifelong badge of honor for each man.

Another nickname evolved in the spring 1862 Valley Campaign. Jackson's insistence on blind obedience to duty and long, rapid marches taxed the men's very existence. Yet they performed superbly. In forty-eight days those Confederates marched more than 670 miles, defeated three different armies, and cleared the Shenandoah Valley of Federal threat. Thereafter, they were "Jackson's Foot Cavalry."

More importantly, the Rockbridge Artillery's John M. Brown wrote proudly, the brigade had "a courage born of good leadership and pride of achievement. They might not shine in dress parade, but their country knew, and the world knew, they were soldiers."

Stuart's Ride Around McClellan

Virginia, June 12–15, 1862 *(following pages)*

Commanding Lee's cavalry in Virginia was twenty-nine-year-old James Ewell Brown Stuart, whom an English observer termed "the perfect picture of a gay cavalier." With a red beard, laughing eyes, and gaudy uniforms, Jeb Stuart proved as superb at information-gathering as he was in battle.

Before Lee could initiate a counteroffensive against McClellan, he needed to know where and how the Union army's right flank was anchored. He dispatched Stuart and 1,200 horsemen on a reconnaissance. Heading out on June 12, 1862, Stuart galloped far to the north, then sliced down behind the Union line. He had no intention of retracing his steps through Federals swarming in his rear. Hence, the Confederates continued

riding—all the way around the Army of the Potomac. Philadelphia field correspondent Joel Cook sneered: "There must have been an awful leak in our lines somewhere."

Stuart returned dramatically to Richmond with 165 prisoners, 260 horses and mules, and valuable information on McClellan's location and strength. His success was achieved at a cost of one fatality. The *Charleston Mercury* exclaimed: "The more we think of Stuart's late feat, the more wonderful it seems." Pvt. Thomas Colley, a farmer in the 1st Virginia Cavalry, proudly wrote home: "We was three days and nights that we was not ought of the saddle. We all stood the trip first rate. . . . We had pretty hard times of it but I would not have missed the trip for $500 as poor a man as I am."

"... They Were Soldiers Indeed"

Lee and Jackson, June 28, 1862, during Seven Days Campaign *(above)*

They were together in the field only eleven months, but Lee and Jackson became as close to a model military partnership as history knows.

In background and personality, they differed markedly. Lee was Virginia aristocracy, an outstanding graduate of West Point, with an unmatched thirty-year career as an army officer. Jackson was an orphan from the western Virginia mountains. He too had graduated from the Military Academy, but succeeded only by sheer determination. The stern, introverted Jackson had spent the 1850s as a professor at the Virginia Military Institute.

To everyone Lee was gracious, charming, exceedingly tactful: an extrovert who balanced patience with devotion to duty. None of these traits existed in Jackson. Shy, humorless, he was totally dedicated to God and to the destruction of the infidels who were invading his native state.

The mutual respect between the two generals was open and deep. Lee said of Jackson: "He is true, honest and brave, has a single eye to the good of the service and spares no exertion to accomplish his object." Jackson stated of the commanding general: "So great is my confidence in General Lee that I am willing to follow him blindfolded."

On the Shoulders of Giants

Lee and Jackson, Frayser's Farm, June 30, 1862 *(below)*

Loud-mouthed Georgia politician Robert Toombs loosed a broadside of disgust at Confederate leadership in the Seven Days Campaign. "Stonewall Jackson and his troops did little or nothing in these battles ... and Lee was far below the occasion."

Several reasons explain why Lee's counteroffensive was not more successful. "But if the enemy was not destroyed," Charles Marshall of Lee's staff wrote in his memoir, paraphrasing Lee's report on the campaign, "the siege of Richmond was raised, and the object of [McClellan's] campaign, which had been prosecuted after months of preparation at an enormous expenditure of men and money, completely frustrated."

The lack of timely and correct information hindered Lee. Sir Frederick Maurice, the distinguished editor of Marshall's memoirs, noted: "The Confederate generals were engaged for the first time in maneuvering a large army, while many of the men were ... little more than recruits. The blunders were many ... but the lessons of the Seven Days were taken to heart by Lee and his generals, and soon bore fruit."

"So great is my confidence in

General Lee that **I am**

willing to follow him

blindfolded."

—Gen. Thomas "Stonewall" Jackson

"I Order You Both to the Rear!"

Gen. A. P. Hill, Pres. Davis, Gen. Lee,
Glendale, Virginia, June 30, 1862

Often, in the heat of battle, decorum melts for the moment. Such occurred on June 30, 1862, as Confederates were making a vicious assault at Glendale. That afternoon Lee, accompanied by President Davis, rode into cannon-range of the battlefield. Gen. A. Powell Hill, the youngest of Lee's division commanders, a Virginian with a reputation for aggressiveness and quick temper, galloped up and shouted: "This is no place for either of you! As commander of this part of the field, I order you both to the rear!"

"We will obey your orders," replied the president with a slight smile. He and Lee rode back a short distance—but not far enough for Hill. Again the red-haired general rode quickly to the pair and angrily demanded that they withdraw to safety. The two officials retired from the field.

In his official report of the battle, Hill mentioned that the president "narrowly escaped accident."

President, This Is Our Stonewall Jackson

Malvern Hill, July 2, 1862

Cordial relations never existed between Jefferson Davis and Thomas Jackson. Early in the war, Davis had received reports that Jackson was a "loose cannon" in the field. The president felt that the former VMI professor was an odd and unpredictable officer who needed a tight leash. Jackson openly resented some of the commander-in-chief's directives, especially during the Romney campaign.

Heavy rain was falling on July 2, 1862, the day after the battle of Malvern Hill. Davis arrived unannounced at Lee's headquarters as the general was conferring with his lieutenants. Lee was taken by surprise. He shook the president's hand, then began introducing his officers. Davis and Jackson had never met. Jackson remained back from the others; and when Davis looked his way inquisitively, Jackson "stood as if a corporal on guard."

Lee saw the two men staring at each other. "Why, President," Lee exclaimed, "don't you know General Jackson? This is our Stonewall Jackson."

The highly sensitive Davis bowed. A staff officer watched the unemotional Jackson give "the salute of an inferior to a superior." No further exchange occurred between the two men.

White House Strategy

Lee, Jackson, and Pres. Davis, Confederate White House, Richmond, Virginia July 13, 1862 *(opposite)*

On July 4, Confederate War Department clerk John B. Jones prophesied: "The commanding general neither sleeps nor slumbers. Already the process of reorganizing Jackson's corps has been commenced for a blow at or near the enemy's capital. Let Lincoln beware the hour of retribution." On a Sunday morning barely ten days after the conclusion of the Peninsula Campaign, Lee and Jackson met with Davis to discuss future strategy. The July 13, 1862, meeting between Davis, Lee, and Jackson is the only known instance when the South's three principal commanders had a private conversation. The two-hour meeting took place in the upstairs office of the president's home—the Confederate White House—which was only four blocks from the capitol building. Since the Davis children had free run of the house, it is likely that five-year-old Jefferson Davis Jr. made an unannounced entrance.

The focal point of the meeting was a new Union threat in Virginia. Gen. John Pope and a Union army were marching south toward the vital rail junction at Gordonsville. The ever-boastful Pope had announced that henceforth his headquarters would be in the saddle. A typical Confederate comment was that "Pope had put his headquarters where his hindquarters ought to be."

Lee made a daring proposal. A sizable portion of his army, under Jackson, would leave the Richmond defenses and proceed to Gordonsville "to observe the enemy's movements closely" and "to avail himself of any opportunity to attack that might arise."

These were challenging words to a general about to lead 11,000 Confederates against 49,500 Federals. Yet Jackson never displayed too much concern about numerical strength. After all, he was sure he had God on his side.

The High Command

Lee and Jackson, Confederate White House, July 13, 1862 *(opposite)*

After their meeting with Pres. Davis, Lee and Jackson mounted their horses and tarried for a moment in front of the presidential mansion. Virginia cavalryman Charles Blackford observed the scene. Lee, Blackford stated, "was elegantly dressed in full uniform . . . and [was] by far the most magnificent man I ever saw." Jackson, on the other hand, "was a typical Roundhead. He was poorly dressed, that is, he looked so though of course his clothes were made of good material. His cap was very indifferent and pulled down over one eye, much stained by weather and without insignia." The dark-suited Davis wore his usual gaunt and rigid expression.

Lee turned east toward his field headquarters. Jackson rode downtown to attend morning services at the Second Presbyterian Church.

"I Will Be Moving within the Hour!"

Jeffersonton, Virginia, August 24, 1862, before Second Manassas *(below)*

Sunday, August 24, was a bright day, with temperatures in the high seventies. Lee's army lay sprawled over the countryside around the village of Jeffersonton.

That afternoon Lee held a conference with his generals. "It was a curious scene," Jackson aide Kyd Douglas recalled. "A table was placed almost in the middle of a field, with not even a tree within hearing. General Lee sat at the table on which was spread a map. General Longstreet sat on his right, General Stuart on his left, and General Jackson stood opposite him."

Lee was going to take a dangerous gamble: abandon the defense of Richmond in order to go after Pope and his menacing army. While Longstreet held Pope's attention along the Rappahannock River, Jackson and 23,500 Southerners would march secretly and swiftly around the Union right flank and cut Pope's communications with Washington. The Federals would likely turn around and hasten back to stop Jackson's threat on the Northern capital. As Pope rushed to fall on Jackson, Lee would pursue the Union army. But for at least forty-eight hours, the two pieces of the Confederate army would be out of touch, and Richmond would be defenseless.

Jackson listened to the plan, stood up, and exclaimed: "I will be moving within [the] hour!"

Decision at Manassas *(right)*
Commanders of Manassas *(below)*

Lee, Jackson, and Longstreet, August 29, 1862

Jackson's flank march averaged a mile and a half per hour for almost two days. "We did not always follow roads," James M. Hendricks of the 2nd Virginia noted, "but went through corn fields and bypaths, waded streams, and occasionally we marched right through someone's yard."

The "foot cavalry" destroyed a portion of the Orange & Alexandria Railroad and burned all of Pope's supplies at Manassas Junction. On August 28, Jackson ambushed part of Pope's marching forces. Battle began in earnest the next day near the old Manassas battleground.

Pope launched a series of uncoordinated—and unsuccessful—attacks on Jackson's entrenched line. The Union general believed that he was casting a net over part of Lee's army. Actually, Pope had marched straight into a net. In the late morning, Longstreet's part of the Confederate army began arriving quietly on Pope's flank.

The Jackson-Pope struggle raged all afternoon. When someone asked Jeb Stuart where Jackson was, the cavalryman smilingly replied: "Where the fighting is hottest!"

Lee and Longstreet found Jackson on high ground overlooking the battle. He quickly explained the situation. Jackson was "pale, serious, and calm," an aide wrote.

Nightfall ended the August 29 combat. Jackson's physician said: "General, we have won this battle by the hardest kind of fighting."

"No, no," Jackson responded gently, "we have won it by the blessing of Almighty God."

Reconnaissance at Manassas

Jackson and Lee, August 31, 1862 *(below)*

It rained throughout the night of August 30 and into the next day. The downpour added to the weariness in the Confederate ranks, and the overcast sky cast a pall over the masses of bodies lying on the Second Manassas battlefield. "I never saw so many dead Yankees before us in my life," North Carolina private Nathan Snead asserted. Lt. John Leslie of New York was equally appalled: "The woods were a sickening sight, strewn with the killed and wounded. In some places they lay in heaps."

Sometime in midmorning, Lee and Jackson rode across Bull Run and through tangled woods to ascertain Pope's position. Enemy fire soon answered the question. As the two generals withdrew to safety, Lee's offensive mind ignited anew. He would send Jackson's troops to try and block the Union retreat.

Jackson listened quietly to Lee's plan. His brigades had been fighting for three days. It was Sunday, the Lord's day. Nevertheless, when Lee finished his instructions, Jackson murmured "Good" and left without a smile.

The subsequent march failed, largely because the "foot cavalry" were too worn out to move swiftly across the rain-soaked countryside.

With a Rebel Yell

Second Manassas, August 29, 1862 *(following pages)*

When Jackson delivered the First Manassas counterattack that won him a lasting nickname, he directed his troops to "yell like furies." The strange and fierce cry they uttered marked the birth of the "rebel yell." It became more widespread—and more varied as the war continued.

Yankee battle shouts were deep, loud, continuous hurrahs and huzzas. The rebel yell was something quite different: a high-pitched, individualistic, staccato sound that many found shrill, jubilant, and savage. The yell had a twofold purpose: to relieve the attacker and to frighten the defender. It succeeded on both counts.

In the August 29 fighting at Second Manassas, the yell was heard at least twice. One instance involved an attack by Gen. Jubal Early's division. To the 17th Virginia's Alexander Hunter, the Confederates, many of whom were foaming at the mouth, appeared momentarily insane: "Over the dead and dying they surged, all the while howling that eerie, inhuman war cry that once heard was never forgotten."

Gods and Generals

Antietam Campaign, Leesburg, Virginia, September 5, 1862

On September 4, Lee wrote President Davis: "I am more fully persuaded of the benefit that will result from an expedition into Maryland. . . . Should the results of the expedition justify it, I propose to enter Pennsylvania, unless you deem it unadvisable upon political or other grounds."

The following day, Lee met with his lieutenants at the Henry Harrison mansion in downtown Leesburg, Virginia. Legend has it that the general first participated in a short religious service in the front parlor. Then, with his army poised to cross

the Potomac River into Maryland, Lee reviewed routes, topography, and points of possible Federal resistance. Paying close attention were Gens. Jackson, Longstreet, Stuart, and Lewis Armistead.

Lee's hands were bandaged as a result of a fall from his horse. Longstreet, suffering from foot blisters, was wearing slippers. Jackson had recently been thrown from his horse and was nursing a sore back. On the eve of the largest battle of the war in the East, the health of the military high command was impaired.

Stonewall Jackson at Harpers Ferry

Virginia, September 15, 1862 · STONEWALL JACKSON AT HARPERS FERRY (*study, below*)

When the large Union garrison at Harpers Ferry, astride Lee's retreat route, did not abandon its position, Lee dispatched Jackson with his three divisions to take the Potomac river town.

The former artillery professor carefully posted fifty cannon on high ground surrounding Harpers Ferry. In the early morning fog of September 15, Jackson began a heavy bombardment. Valleys echoed as if "many volcanoes" had exploded at one time. Inside the town, recalled Ohio colonel William H. Trimble, "the [fire] commanded every foot of it around the batteries . . . producing a terrible cross-fire. . . . There was not a place where you could lay the palm of your hand and say it was safe."

Within an hour, the garrison surrendered. Jackson seized 12,500 prisoners, 73 cannon, 13,000 small arms, 200 wagons, and 1,200 mules. The general rode triumphantly into town. Large numbers of Union prisoners saluted or cheered Jackson. South Carolina soldier James Caldwell stated: "The general gave a stiff acknowledgement of the compliment, pulled down his hat, drove spurs into his horse, and went clattering down the hill away from the noise."

Near midnight, Jackson and two of his divisions started northward to rejoin Lee at the village of Sharpsburg, Maryland.

Jackson at Antietam

Dunker Church, Sharpsburg, Maryland, September 17, 1862

The killing began at dawn. A humid Wednesday, September 17, 1862, proved to be the bloodiest day in the nation's history. The first four hours in the thirteen hours of fighting at Antietam centered on Jackson's sector of the Confederate line.

Woods and a large cornfield became a vast arena as soldiers blue and gray struggled savagely. At the first collision, Wisconsin soldier Rufus Dawes exclaimed, "The hostile battle lines opened a tremendous fire upon each other. Men . . . were knocked out of the ranks by dozens." Later, a member of the 4th Texas called the action "the hottest place I ever saw on this earth or want to see hereafter."

Troops of two Union corps pounded Jackson's defenses. The general earned anew the nickname "Stonewall." His lines bent, and bent some more, but never broke. By midmorning, when battle shifted to the east, Jackson had lost 40 percent of his command. (The famous Stonewall Brigade was down to the size of two companies rather than the normal fifty.) Union casualties exceeded 12,000 soldiers.

Jackson was concerned but calm throughout the fighting. He was convinced, a fellow general later recounted, that "God would protect him and no harm would befall him."

Raise the Colors and Follow Me!

The Irish Brigade at Antietam, September 17, 1862

Thomas Francis Meagher won fame as a patriot in an unsuccessful 1848 uprising in Ireland. He came to America, saw a similar struggle for freedom, and in 1861 joined the Union army. With the backing of the Catholic archbishop of New York, Meagher organized an all-Irish brigade that bore distinctively green regimental flags. The hard-drinking, witty, and brave Meagher was the epitome of a dashing Irish soldier.

At Antietam, heavy Confederate fire from a sunken road pinned down the Irishmen. "Men on both sides fell in large numbers every moment," Capt. David Conyngham of the brigade

staff wrote, "and those who were eye-witnesses of the struggle did not suppose it possible for a single man to escape."

The only exit, Meagher concluded, was straight ahead. Then Meagher stood up in the stirrups, raised his sword high, and shouted: "Boys! Raise the colors and follow me!"

Irish soldiers cheered and surged forward. Southerners in the road unleashed a volley that took down half of the 63rd New York. Ten color-bearers fell in rapid succession. Seventy-five of 120 newly arrived recruits were killed or wounded. Meagher was knocked unconscious in the action. The Irish advance ended 100 yards from the sunken road because the men ran out of ammunition.

Hancock the Superb

The Irish Brigade at Antietam, September 17, 1862

Irish Brigade general Thomas Meagher and division commander Israel Richardson both went down during the fight for the sunken road at Antietam. Winfield Scott Hancock quickly stepped into the leadership vacuum. Valor in the spring 1862 Peninsula Campaign had led McClellan to call him "Hancock the Superb." Now he proved again his worthiness as a combat officer. Hancock gathered fragments of units (including the 69th New York pictured here) and kept the Union line unbroken for the rest of the action.

At thirty-nine, unusually tall, Hancock was an officer of magnetic presence. He always wore a clean white shirt, and he possessed a bull voice usually laced with profanity. A lieutenant found Hancock in battle "superb and calm, as on review, imperturbable, self-evident." Another Union soldier put it simply: "One felt safe when near him."

Sharpsburg War Council

September 17, 1862

A somber air hung over the meeting of Lee and his lieutenants on the night after Antietam. A worn-out James Graham of the 27th North Carolina wrote that "the sun seemed almost to go backwards" that day, "and it appeared as if night would never come."

The northern invasion had failed. McClellan's Union army still loomed across the way. Only two-thirds of Lee's forces remained to fight. The Confederates were too weak to attack, too proud to run. Lee would wait and see if McClellan renewed the struggle the next morning.

His lieutenants listened attentively as Lee discussed options for the next day. When James Longstreet arrived late at the meeting, Lee looked up and said: "Ah, here is Longstreet; here is my old war horse."

Longstreet is leaning over the table. Behind him are two of Lee's lieutenant generals: John B. Hood with hat in hand and Daniel Harvey Hill holding a hand to his chin. Lee stands in the center, his hand still bandaged from a fall he had a few weeks earlier. At the far right stands Jackson, one foot on a table brace. Jubal Early is behind Jackson. Powell Hill is smoking his pipe.

Late the next day Lee ordered a withdrawal to Virginia. Jackson observed: "It is better to have fought the battle in Maryland than to have left it without a struggle."

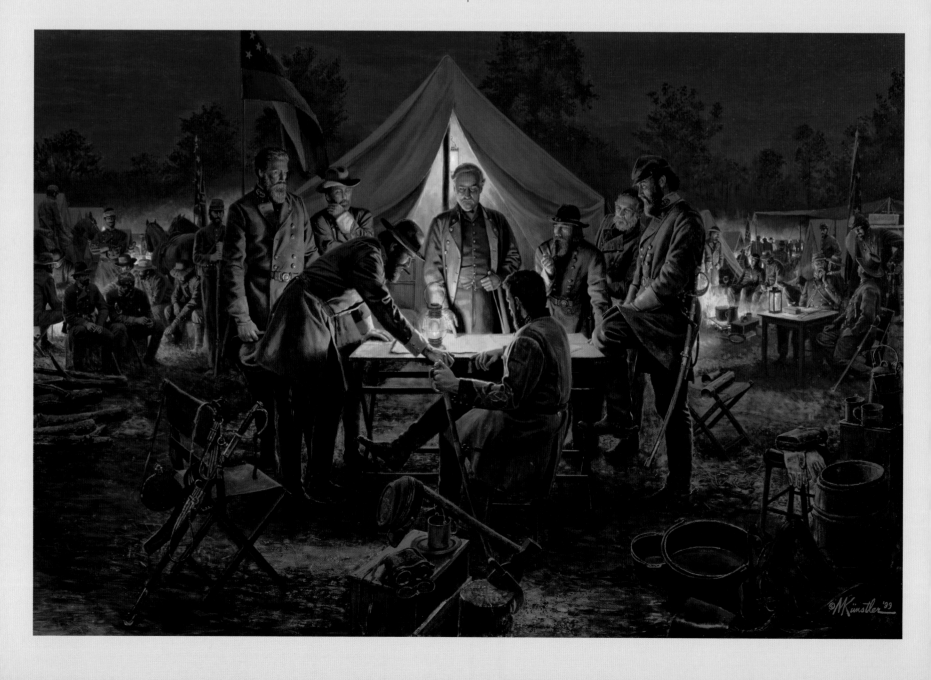

Night Crossing

Lee and Jackson, September 19, 1862 · NIGHT CROSSING (study, below)

Lee abandoned the Antietam lines on the night of September 18 and started back to Virginia. Throughout the next day his army crossed the Potomac at Boteler's Ford, a point where the river was mostly knee-deep.

Near sunset a thunderstorm saturated the ground and turned the banks of the Potomac into mud. The retreating column slowed to a crawl. A Union attack at that moment could have been lethal. Staff officer Henry P. L. King termed the traffic jam at the river "an immense mass of troops and wagons of all descriptions." When Jackson's artillery began to bog down, Jackson's quartermaster, Maj. John Harman, rode into the stream and unleashed a stream of profanity that sent men and beasts quickly toward the opposite bank.

The last foot soldiers crossed the Potomac to safety. A relieved Lee was heard to murmur: "Thank God."

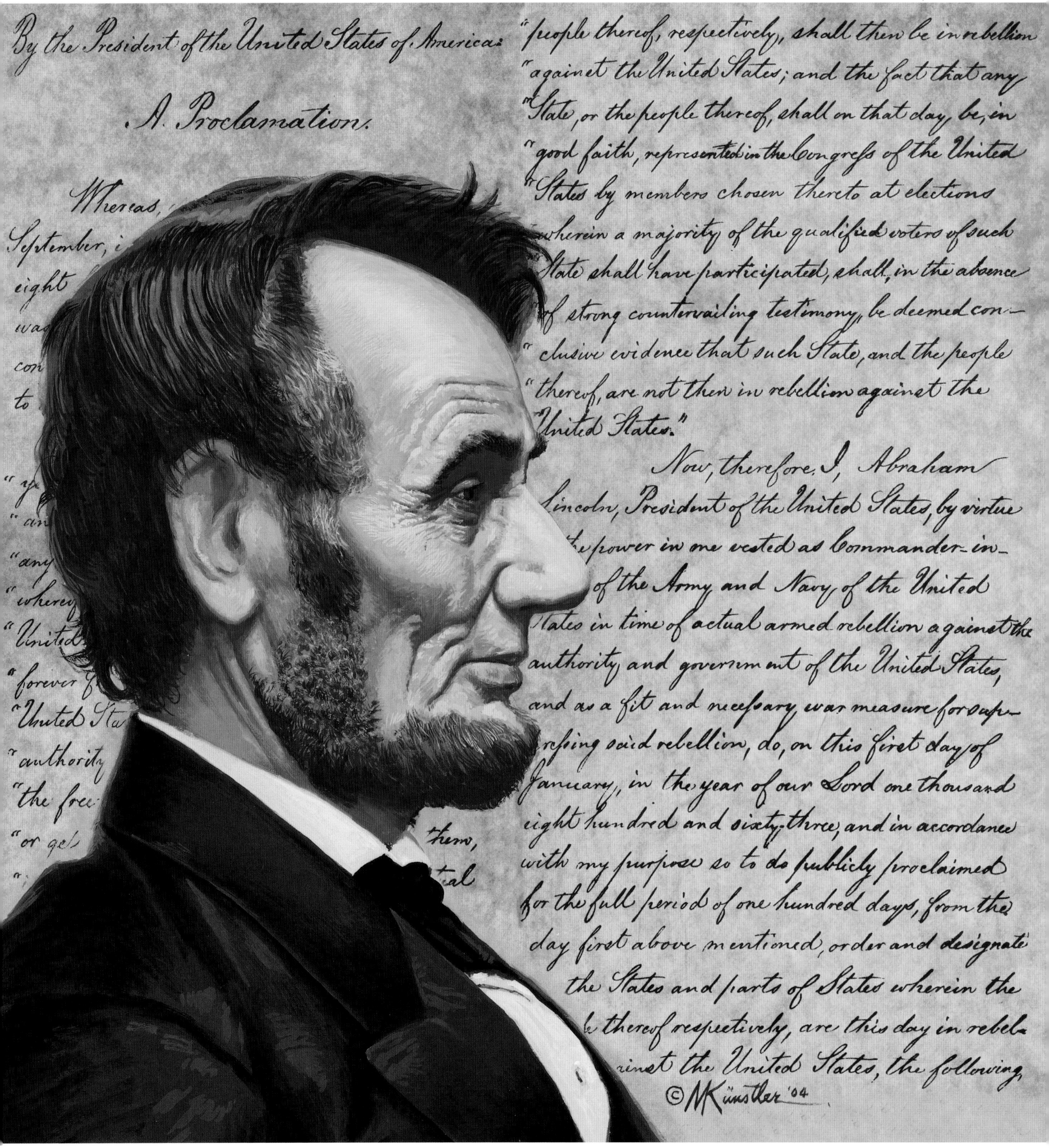

By the President of the United States of America:

A Proclamation.

Whereas,
September, i
eight
wa
con
to

"if
"an
"any
"whereu
"United
"forever
"United Sta
"authority
"the free
"or gen

them,

tal

"people thereof, respectively, shall then be in rebellion
"against the United States; and the fact that any
"State, or the people thereof, shall on that day be, in
"good faith, represented in the Congress of the United
"States by members chosen thereto at elections
"wherein a majority of the qualified voters of such
"State shall have participated, shall, in the absence
"of strong countervailing testimony, be deemed con—
"clusive evidence that such State, and the people
"thereof, are not then in rebellion against the
"United States."

Now, therefore, I, Abraham
Lincoln, President of the United States, by virtue
the power in me vested as Commander-in-
of the Army and Navy, of the United
States in time of actual armed rebellion against the
authority and government of the United States,
and as a fit and necessary war measure for sup-
pressing said rebellion, do, on this first day of
January, in the year of our Lord one thousand
eight hundred and sixty-three, and in accordance
with my purpose so to do publicly proclaimed
for the full period of one hundred days, from the
day first above mentioned, order and designate
the States and parts of States wherein the
thereof respectively, are this day in rebel-
inst the United States, the following

©Künstler '04

"The fiery trial through which we pass, will light us down, in honor or

dishonor, to the latest generation. . . . **In giving freedom to**

the slave, we assure freedom to the free—

honorable alike in what we give, and what we preserve.

We shall nobly save, or meanly lose, the last best, hope of earth."

—Pres. Abraham Lincoln,
address to U.S. Congress, December 1, 1862

Emancipation Proclamation (Portrait)

September 22, 1862

Abraham Lincoln repeatedly stated in the first year of the Civil War that reunion was the most and the least he had ever asked as president. Yet as one bloody season followed another, Lincoln saw that the necessities of war were demanding more than he had expected. He must go beyond saving the Union. Reunion could not occur without settling once and for all the issue of slavery.

To act on the subject, Lincoln had to wait for a military victory so that his announcement could be presented from a position of strength. Antietam gave him the opportunity. Four days after the battle, Lincoln issued a preliminary Emancipation Proclamation. All slaves in a state or part of a state still in rebellion as of January 1, 1863, would be "thenceforward, and forever, free."

The document had many weak points. Lincoln issued the Emancipation Proclamation not as president but as commander in chief of armed forces. It was therefore a military measure involving what became a social revolution. The edict applied only to slaves in states still in rebellion as of January 1, 1863. (It said nothing about slaves in such areas as Kentucky and Maryland.) Further, the document's constitutionality was widely in question. On the other hand, it blocked any intervention in the war by England or France because the Civil War was hereafter to be a contest for union *and* freedom. The Emancipation Proclamation showed the Confederate States how much they stood to lose by continuing to fight. It proclaimed that America and freedom were thereafter to be the same thing.

Lincoln made his position clear when he told the Congress in his State of the Union address on December 1: "In giving freedom to the slave, we assure freedom to the free—honorable alike in what we give, and what we preserve. We shall nobly save, or meanly lose, the last best, hope of earth."

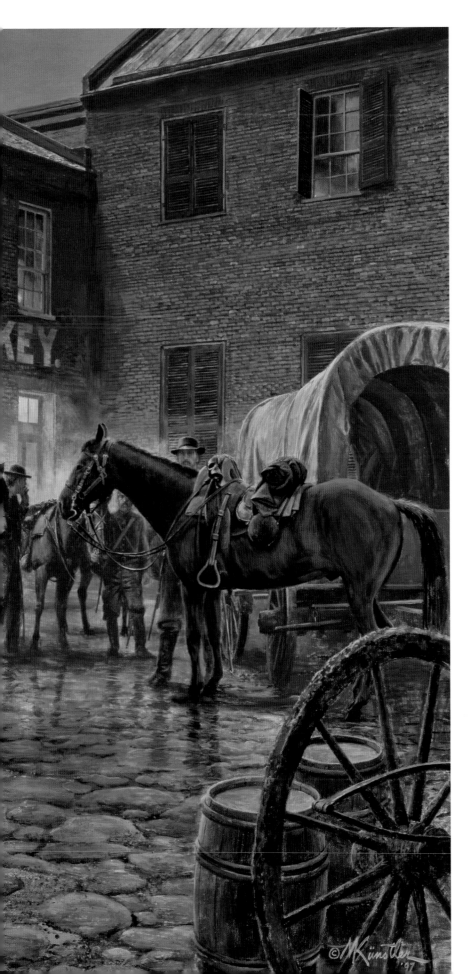

The Palace Bar

Winchester, Virginia, October 18, 1862

Jackson's men returned from Antietam and reestablished camps around Winchester. This allowed them to recuperate from battle while guarding the northern gateway to the Shenandoah Valley. Local citizens welcomed them home.

A troop of cavalry passed through Winchester on a rainy night in October. While the horsemen pause at one of the town's favorite saloons, a young officer and his sweetheart share a precious embrace.

Winchester residents lived in uncertainty. Forty-year-old Laura Lee wrote at this time: "Sad and dreary is the prospect before us, in being separated from our friends and unable to hear any true accounts."

"**Sad and dreary** is the prospect before us, in being separated from our friends and **unable to hear any true accounts.**"

—Laura Lee, Winchester resident

Shenandoah Autumn

Gens. Stuart and Jackson, Millwood, Virginia, November 4, 1862

Stonewall Jackson and Jeb Stuart seemed on the surface to have nothing in common. Jackson was a stern Calvinist, introspective and humorless. Stuart was a buoyant cavalier, extroverted and fun-loving. Stuart was the only man who dared to kid Jackson and the only person with whom Jackson ever attempted humor. Aggressive leadership and profound faith not only bound the two generals but kindled a deep friendship.

Late on the night of November 4, Stuart arrived at Jackson's headquarters, Carter Hall, Col. Nathaniel Burwell's imposing home east of Winchester. Jackson was asleep. Stuart crawled into bed with him and apparently got control of most of the covers.

The next morning, enjoying a hearty breakfast, Jackson said to Stuart: "I am always glad to see you." Jackson began rubbing his legs and added: "But, General, you must not get into my bed with your boots and spurs on and ride me around like a cavalry horse all night!"

Stuart was still laughing when he mounted his horse and bade his friend goodbye.

Lee at Fredericksburg

Princess Anne Street, 9:40 AM, November 20, 1862

Fredericksburg stood at the fall line of the Rappahannock River and was midway between the opposing capitals of Washington and Richmond.

Lincoln's patience with the ever-vacillating McClellan ran out early in November. Lincoln replaced him with Gen. Ambrose E. Burnside, who immediately moved to get around Lee's right flank and force a battle in the open country south of Fredericksburg.

The Union advance stalled. Lee shifted his forces to the high ground behind the city. His army was in poor physical shape. "We are a dirty, ragged set, mother," Georgian soldier Theodore Fogle wrote his mother, "but courage & heroism find many a true disciple among us."

On November 20, a somber Lee rode into Fredericksburg. Beside him was Longstreet. Directly under the flag is Col. Charles Marshall, Lee's aide-de-camp. Medical director Lafayette Guild is the caped rider behind and to Lee's right. Townspeople greeted Lee's arrival with a mixture of surprise, joy, and anxiety.

"We are a dirty, ragged set, mother, but courage & heroism find many a true disciple among us."

—Theodore Fogle, 2nd Georgia

Strategy in the Snow

Fredericksburg, Virginia, November 29, 1862 *(opposite)*

When Burnside's intentions to cross the Rappahannock became obvious, Lee summoned Jackson to move his corps from the Shenandoah Valley and join the other half of the army at Fredericksburg. Battle was imminent, Lee reported. Jackson's corps would occupy the Confederate right while Longstreet's command held the left.

Late one afternoon, Jackson received word that Lee wished to see him at headquarters. The next morning, with snow and subfreezing winds blowing, Jackson began the thirteen-mile trip. It took all day. Lee was both surprised and a little angry to see Jackson. "General," he said, "you know I did not wish you to come in such a storm. It was a matter of little importance. I am sorry that you had that ride."

Jackson blushed, then with a hint of a smile replied: "I received your note, General Lee."

Remember Me

Fredericksburg, November 30, 1862 *(above)*

Fredericksburg had been one of the most beautiful towns in Virginia. Evan Woodward of the 3rd Pennsylvania Reserves remembered it as "an ancient city . . . and principally known for the refinement of its inhabitants, their aristocratic characteristics and the beauty of its women."

By early December 1862, Fredericksburg was a no-man's land caught between two armies massing for battle on opposite banks of the Rappahannock River. Hundreds of citizens had abandoned the town. Confederate soldiers took their places. The place was looking dirty and unwanted.

A few buildings still retained their charm. St. George's Episcopal Church was the area's most elaborate example of the Romanesque architectural style. Built in 1849, its steeple was the city landmark. The church bell could be heard throughout the town. In the last half of the war, the bullet-riddled building was a hospital for Union soldiers wounded in nearby engagements.

The Fighting 69th

Gen. Meagher and the Irish Brigade—Fredericksburg, December 2, 1862

The "Fighting 69th" New York was part of Gen. Thomas Meagher's Irish Brigade. Heavy casualties at Antietam had dampened neither its pride nor its determination. The regiment arrived at Fredericksburg and took its place amid the sprawling camps on the north side of the Rappahannock River.

A staff officer is pointing out to Meagher that the long-awaited pontoon bridges are finally at hand. Behind the general are the Irish Brigade flag and a bullet-riddled Stars and Stripes. The tattered 69th battle flag had been sent home to New York for replacement. "To show the green" in the forthcoming battle, the men of the 69th would wear sprigs of boxwood tucked in their kepis.

"The brigade never was in finer spirit and condition," Meagher reported, "and it would be difficult to say whether those who were to be led, or those who were to lead, were the better prepared or the more eager to discharge their duty."

Changing of the Pickets

Fredericksburg, December 6, 1862

To avoid provoking enemy fire on Fredericksburg, Lee kept only a line of pickets (advance guards) in the downtown area. This scene vividly shows the Episcopal and Presbyterian churches as well as the courthouse buildings. Changing of the picket guard is taking place while residents who still remain in town gather for evening services.

The soldiers' presence naturally attracts attention. Two young boys venture to strike up a conversation with a courier.

Ambrose Burnside's army seemed incapable of getting across the Rappahannock. Fresh snow covered the ground. A Southern picket announced confidently to his parents: "I think myself the campaign is over." Meanwhile, Burnside continued to make plans for what he thought would be "the most decisive battle of the war."

Scouts of Fredericksburg *(below, right)* • "...So Close to the Enemy" *(bottom)*

Maj. Von Borcke with Gens. Lee and Jackson, Fredericksburg, December 12, 1862

Lee and Jackson were as bold in person as they were in battle. By midday of December 12, Confederates were massed along a seven-mile front at Fredericksburg. To obtain a better look at the enemy's intentions, the two Southern generals, accompanied by several aides, rode out ahead of their lines. They dismounted, left their horses with the aides, and walked stealthily through snow-covered woods. From there, they could easily see the Union positions 400 yards away.

Maj. Heros von Borcke of Stuart's staff retired twenty yards to the rear to give the generals privacy during their conference. He grew increasingly nervous at "the two greatest generals of the war" being so close to Union lines. "One well-directed shot, or a

rapid dash of resolute horsemen," von Borcke thought, "might have destroyed the hopes and confidence of our whole army."

After "many minutes of painful anxiety and impatience" among the waiting staff officers, Lee and Jackson returned to their horses.

Lee's Lieutenants

High Command at Fredericksburg, December 13, 1862

Saturday, December 13, 1862, dawned in heavy fog. Battle would be delayed.

A confident Jackson was "in his most serene and cheerful mood," aide Kyd Douglas noticed. Yet he did not look like himself. In place of the old weather-beaten uniform by which soldiers knew him, "Old Jack" was wearing a gold-laced coat, a personal gift from Stuart. He also was attired in new trousers and cap, shiny boots, plus new saber and spurs—all sent to him by grateful admirers.

Jackson rode down his lines. At first the soldiers did not recognize him. Then hoots and laughter began. One private shouted: "Come here, boys! Stonewall has drawed his bounty and has bought himself some new clothes!" Another did not think it natural that the general was "dressed up as fine as a Lieutenant or a Quartermaster." Through it all, Jackson blushed.

Stuart, Lee, Jackson, and Longstreet riding together a short time later brought the loudest cheering. The quartet represented the soul of the Army of Northern Virginia. Notice that none of the soldiers' faces is visible. They all were looking proudly at the four generals who controlled their destiny.

The Professor and His Tutor

Lt. Col. Chamberlain and Col. Ames, 20th Maine

Lawrence Chamberlain's intellect led to his appointment as lieutenant colonel of the 20th Maine. The colonel was Adelbert Ames, an 1861 graduate of West Point and wounded hero at First Manassas. Ames took one look at the 900 fishermen, farmers, and lumbermen he was to lead—only two were in uniform—and exclaimed in disgust: "This is a hell of a regiment!"

Chamberlain and Ames became more than instant friends. The young colonel became a military tutor to the former professor who had never commanded anything larger than a classroom. At every opportunity the two men huddled in intensive study of army regulations, strategy, and tactics. "I *study*, I tell you, every military work I can find," Chamberlain wrote his wife. "It is no small labor to master the evolutions of a Battalion & Brigade."

The solemn ex-teacher proved an eager student who absorbed his lessons well.

Lt. Col. J. L. Chamberlain and Staff

Fredericksburg, December 13, 1862

By the time of the battle of Fredericksburg, professor-turned-soldier Lawrence Chamberlain was showing distinct promise as a regimental leader, though his 20th Maine had seen no action.

Chamberlain watched anxiously as his regiment crossed the Rappahannock. "The enemy's cannoneers knew the ranges perfectly," he wrote. "The air was thick with the flying, bursting shells; whooping solid shot swept lengthwise our narrow bridge . . . driving the compressed air so close to our heads that there was an unconquerable instinct to shrink beneath it."

"... War Is So Terrible"

Longstreet & Lee, Fredericksburg, December 13, 1862 · "... WAR IS SO TERRIBLE" *(study, right)*

The sheer vastness of the Union army concentrated below him at Fredericksburg gave Lee some initial concerns. Early in the contest he said to Longstreet: "They are massing very heavily and will break your line."

Longstreet gave a grunt. "General," he snarled, "if you put every man on the other side of the Potomac in that field to approach me over that same line, and give me plenty of ammunition, I will kill them all before they reach my line!"

A Union assault on Jackson's position on the low ground near Hamilton's Crossing made a momentary breakthrough. Jackson poured heavy reinforcements into the breach. Union ranks suffered as many casualties rushing away from the battlefield—dubbed the "Slaughter Pen"—as they did in making the attack.

Lee quietly watched the action. At the Union repulse, he stated: "It is well that war is so terrible; else we should grow too fond of it."

In the Hands of Providence

The 20th Maine, Fredericksburg, December 13, 1862

All day the 20th Maine had waited out of gun range and listened to the roaring sounds of death. Shortly after 3 p.m., the order came for the men to advance onto the battleground. This last assault would seek to establish a stable line on the field where waves of Federals had swept back and forth in futile attacks.

Ames and Chamberlain led the New Englanders across the plain under heavy fire from the enemy. A Federal on the front line watched the 20th Maine "coming across the field in line of battle, as upon parade, easily recognized by their new state colors, the great gaps plainly visible as the shot and shell tore through the now tremulous line. It was a grand sight, and a striking example of what discipline will do for *such* material in *such* a battle."

The regiment struggled to the ridge that was its objective just as darkness descended.

" It was a grand sight, and a

striking example of

what discipline will do

for SUCH material in SUCH a battle."

—Pvt. Robert Goldthwaite Carter,
22nd Massachusetts

Valor in Gray

Kershaw's Brigade at Fredericksburg, December 13, 1862

All afternoon of the thirteenth, Union lines kept attacking—and kept melting away under the withering cannon fire from atop Marye's Heights and rifle fire from infantry packed below behind a stone wall. Gen. Joseph Kershaw and his South Carolina brigade stood four deep behind the wall.

His veterans kept firing while the men behind them loaded rifles and passed them forward. "Their fire," Kershaw stated in his official report, "was the most rapid and continuous I have ever witnessed, [and] not a man was wounded by the fire of his own comrades." Artillery in support were firing fifty shells per minute.

Confederates used their shirts to swab weapons clean during the intense action. Gunpowder smeared their faces. The constant shooting had its effect on the Carolinians. "Our shoulders were kicked blue by the muskets," one stated.

The battlefield came to resemble a blood-soaked blanket of blue. No Federal soldier ever got closer than twenty-five yards to the wall. George Washburn of the 108th New York said it bluntly: "We might as well have tried to take Hell."

Courage in Blue

Chamberlain at Fredericksburg, December 13, 1862

An observer watched the Union assaults at Fredericksburg in wonder: "Their devotion transcended anything I ever saw or even dreamed about. Men walked right up to their deaths as though it were to a feast."

Lt. Col. Chamberlain and his 20th Maine were in the final charge. They surged forward with other units across the half-mile open plain. From the first line of Union wounded came shouts: "It's no use, boys, we've tried that! Nothing living can stand there! It's only for the dead!"

Chamberlain remembered trampling "over bodies of dead men and living ones, past four lines that were lying on the ground." Another soldier recalled: "The groans of the dying and wounded soldiers when trodden on were heartrending in the extreme." Men lay "weltering in their gore."

Pinned down by intense fire for two nights and a day, the Maine troops used corpses for protection. Gen. James Longstreet, whose troops repulsed the Union attacks, stated: "A series of braver, more desperate charges than those hurled against our troops . . . was never known."

"Angel of Marye's Heights"

Sgt. Richard Kirkland, Fredericksburg, December 14, 1862

"No one dared to go to the relief of the wounded," New York infantryman Richard Connor stated the day after the battle, "because the appearance of a head above the breastworks was the signal for a volley."

Richard Kirkland was twenty years old and a sergeant in the 2nd South Carolina. His regiment had been one of the units defending that impenetrable stone wall. The morning after the battle, Kirkland could no longer tolerate the cries for water from the battlefield. He obtained permission from Gen. Kershaw to take water to the wounded.

The young Confederate climbed over the wall with a half-dozen canteens. For close to two hours, he went back and forth for water while ministering to injured Federal soldiers all over the field. Friend and foe alike silently watched Kirkland's acts of mercy. "Such deeds as this," a Union soldier declared, "are the redeeming features of war."

Thereafter, the Carolinian was known as the "Angel of Marye's Heights." Nine months after Fredericksburg, Kirkland died on September 20, 1863, in the fighting at Chickamauga, Georgia.

"Such deeds as this are the redeeming features of the war."

—Union soldier on Richard Kirkland

The Angel of the Battlefield

Clara Barton with Walt Whitman at Chatham, Fredericksburg, December 15, 1862 *(following pages)*

The Lacy House ("Chatham," it was often called) was a stately mansion that overlooked the Rappahannock River and Fredericksburg. Numbered among its visitors were Washington, Jefferson, Lee, and Lincoln. Yet the home knew its darkest hours when it became a field hospital for untold numbers of Union and a number of Confederate casualties from the nearby battle at Fredericksburg. No fewer than 1,200 wounded men were packed into the rooms and hallways of the mansion. (Five soldiers were stuffed onto the four shelves of the kitchen cabinet.)

Late arrivals from the battlefield lay on the cold, muddy ground. Moving among the wounded troops was a forty-one-year-old volunteer nurse named Clara Barton. She seemed to be everywhere: distributing food, applying bandages, showing kindness to what she called "hundreds of the worst wounded men I have ever seen."

Similar feats after other engagements earned Miss Barton the title of the "Angel of the Battlefield." Her best biographer, Stephen Oates, asserted that the nurse's experiences at Fredericksburg "would haunt her through all her remaining years."

Another nurse at the Lacy House was Walt Whitman. The bearded poet *(right)* is seen giving water to a Union soldier. Whitman was stunned by the crowded and chaotic situation he beheld. "Everything impromptu, no system … all the wounds pretty bad, some frightful, the men in their old clothes, unclean and bloody."

My Friend, the Enemy

Rappahannock River, Virginia,
December 25, 1862

Fraternization was ever-present in the war. This was not remarkable. Johnny Rebs and Billy Yanks spoke the same language, had the same backgrounds and cultures, possessed the same likes and dislikes. While it was easy to hate the enemy in abstract, sometimes individual feelings overcame sectional animosity.

Opposing soldiers learned that burying the dead together made the odious task easier. Pickets often struck truces out of logic: their individual deaths were not going to alter the outcome of the war, and monotonous patrols became more bearable once the element of death was removed.

A regular reason for fraternization was the Federals' wish for tobacco and the Confederates' desire for coffee. This swapping of hard-to-get items is shown here as two enemy soldiers meet in the Rappahannock River. They had declared a truce by long-distance shouting. Now they stand in no-man's land and silently enjoy luxuries for a few moments.

Winston Churchill once dubbed the American Civil War "the last war between gentlemen."

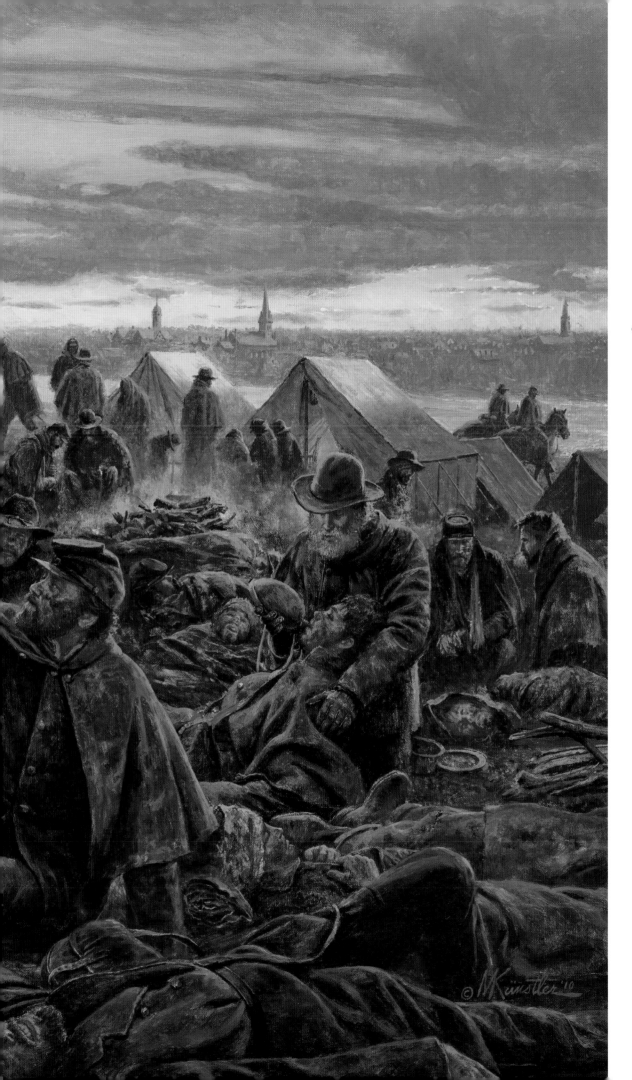

"I cannot tell you the number, but some **hundreds** **of the worst** **wounded men** **I have ever seen** were lying on a little hay on floors or in tents."

—Clara Barton

"Merry Christmas, General Lee!"

Moss Neck, Fredericksburg, December 25, 1862

Richard Corbin's plantation consisted of 1,600 acres several miles downriver from Fredericksburg. The main house on the Moss Neck estate was patterned after an English country residence, stood on high ground, and was 250 feet long from wing to wing.

Jackson established his 1862–63 winter headquarters in a small wooden office building fifty yards from the main house. He quickly received so much food from grateful citizens that he invited Lee and several other generals to a Christmas dinner. The affair blended the happiness of a recent victory with the yuletide spirit.

Lee was departing for camp just as guests began arriving for an evening party hosted by the Corbins. Unquestionably, several of the admirers shouted: "Merry Christmas, General Lee!"

The commander, in his humble way, would have bowed from the saddle and tipped his hat.

Janie Corbin and "Old Jack"

Moss Neck, Fredericksburg, Winter 1862

Jackson enjoyed the winter months at Moss Neck. As an unloved orphan, he always had a deep fondness for children. The desire to see his newborn daughter added to the attraction that developed between the general and six-year-old Janie Corbin.

The child quickly captured his heart. Aide J. P. Smith described Janie as "very pretty and bright, and as happy and sunny a child as I ever saw. She . . . was the general's delight."

Every afternoon Jackson would take time to play with Janie and listen to her childish prattle. Staff officers were amazed at the sight. One moment their rigid and humorless commander was saying of the enemy: "We must do more than defeat their armies; we must destroy them." The next moment, he was a tender father-figure romping happily with the small child.

Morgan's Raiders

Alexandria, Tennessee, December 21, 1862

In the West and only a week after his December 14 wedding, Kentuckian general John Hunt Morgan embarked on his third raid into Northern-held territory. Because of Morgan's previous exploits, 20,400 Federals had been diverted from field operations to guard the communication and supply lines Morgan enjoyed destroying.

A prewar hemp manufacturer in Lexington, Kentucky, Morgan became a brigadier general in command of partisan rangers or irregulars—organized soldiers who practiced partisan or guerrilla tactics. His specialty was hit-and-run tactics, which Morgan and his Kentucky Cavaliers honed, bringing guerrilla warfare to a new peak.

Morgan's Christmas raid was designed to sever all links between the Union army in middle Tennessee and its supply base at Louisville, Kentucky. Morgan and 4,000 superb horsemen—"the pick of the youth of Kentucky," one officer asserted—traveled light and moved with lightning speed. Over the next fourteen days, the Confederates rode 500 miles, inflicted 150 casualties, captured 1,800 Federals, burned 2,290 feet of railroad bridgework, and wrecked 35 miles of rail line. Morgan lost two killed and twenty-four wounded. "Our success far exceeded my expectation," Morgan confessed to his bride. The *Cincinnati Gazette* saw it differently. It termed Morgan "one of the greatest scoundrels that ever went unhung."

Emancipation Proclamation

White House, Washington, D.C., January 1, 1863

Lincoln's cabinet members were the only witnesses when the president signed into law the Emancipation Proclamation on New Year's Day, 1863. Seated with Lincoln is Secretary of the Navy Gideon Welles. Immediately behind the president is Secretary of War Edwin M. Stanton. Secretary of State William H. Seward stands at the far right.

"If my name ever goes into history," Lincoln told his cabinet, "it will be for this act, and my whole soul is in it."

Lincoln took a bold risk in declaring the war to be a social revolution as well, but he was convinced that the nation had to take a meaningful step forward by making American democracy untainted by human bondage. The contest was no longer only to erase a boundary line from the map. Henceforth, it would also be a war fought to erase a word—slavery—from the American experience.

An aged slave preacher described emancipation in simple prayer: "Lord, we ain't what we oughta be. We ain't what we want to be. We ain't what we goin' to be. But, thank God, we ain't what we was."

The Gray Ghost

Mosby's Rangers, Warrenton, Virginia January 18, 1863 *(opposite)*

Having proven himself in 1861–62 as an extraordinary scout for Lee's army, John S. Mosby then received authorization for a small independent command to operate behind Union lines in northern Virginia. The unit became Mosby's Rangers; its leader—small, thin, as restless as he was fearless—would be called the Gray Ghost of the Confederacy.

On the icy evening of January 18, 1863, Mosby and the nucleus of his new battalion passed through Warrenton, Virginia. The county courthouse building stands out in the darkness, as does the warmth of the nearby hotel. It was a quiet beginning of a legendary group of cavalrymen. By war's end, a Virginia citizen would describe Mosby's men as having "all the glamour of Robin Hood, all the courage and bravery of the ancient crusaders, the unexpectedness of the benevolent pirates and the stealth of Indians."

The Mud March

Rappahannock Riverside, Virginia, January 20–22, 1863 (*previous pages*)

Burnside's second attempt to "strike a great and mortal blow to the rebellion" met with another humiliating defeat—not from Lee but from Mother Nature.

A month after the debacle at Fredericksburg, Burnside began a swift march up the Rappahannock to cross the river beyond Lee's left flank and come at the Southerners from the rear. The first day's march went well; then three days of icy rain and swirling wind—from January 20 to 22—turned the countryside into bottomless mud.

Vermont soldier Wilbur Fiske wrote a penetrating account of the "Mud March": The effort "means to the soldiers wet feet every day of the march, the cold ground to lie upon, and insufficient food. . . . It means coughs, cold, consumptions, rheumatism, and fevers, a row of unmarked graves all along the track of the army, and desolation and mourning in thousands of pleasant homes.

It means the pain of seeing in every company brave fellows sinking right down to death before your eyes, with no possibility of helping them, or even doing much to soothe their last hours.

"It means, if battle comes, the wounded left to freeze in the severity of the nights, or to mingle their blood with the deep mud on which they lie. It means every possible form of human suffering, privation, and hardship. Make allowances for us, then, and pray for our strength, endurance, and success, and drop a tear over the brave fellows who are sacrificed, not merely to demon battle, but to the more dreaded severities of the winter season."

Review at Moss Neck

Fredericksburg, Virginia, January 21, 1863 (*below*)

Jackson spent most of January at the Corbin mansion in Moss Neck, writing battle reports and enjoying the company of Janie Corbin.

On his birthday, January 21, Jackson accompanied Lee on a review of a cavalry brigade formed in the front yard of the Corbin estate. To Jackson's right is Gen. W. H. F. "Rooney" Lee, Robert E. Lee's son and leader of the brigade being reviewed. Jeb Stuart is mounted on Lee's left, while Longstreet is behind the two.

The condition of this troop is deceiving. Lee's army was in dreadful condition. Two days after this inspection, Lee informed President Davis that his "greatest uneasiness" was lack of supplies. "I fear the efficiency of the army will be reduced by thousands of men," Lee warned.

Many soldiers had no shoes, blankets, socks, or underwear. Virtually every regiment lacked a full complement of arms. Hunger was ever-present. And another campaign loomed with the coming of spring.

Model Partnership

Jackson and Lee

It was indeed a model partnership. Bound by a common cause and common faith, Lee and Jackson acted not as superior and subordinate, but as equals with a single purpose.

Viscount Wolseley of the British army met them both during the war. "The feelings of the soldiers for General Lee," he discovered, "resembles . . . a fixed and unshakable faith in all he did, and a calm confidence in victory when serving under him." On the other hand, Jackson "is idolised with that intense fervour which, consisting of mingled personal attachment and devoted loyalty, causes them to meet death for his sake, and bless him when dying."

Lee's Lieutenants *(study, top, left)*

Jackson, Lee, and Longstreet

The fortunes of the Army of Northern Virginia during 1862–63 revolved around three different generals with different personalities.

Richmond editor Edward Pollard thought Jackson (foreground) "challenged comparison with the most extraordinary phenomena in the annals of military genius." Jackson's silent nature and deep piety set him apart from others. His West Point classmate, Union general George McClellan, once confessed: "I don't like Jackson's movements; he will appear suddenly when least expected."

Lee (center) was the patriarchal commander whose presence bred respect. Lee's "perceptions are as quick and unerring as his judgment is infallible," Jackson once declared. Lee's aide Lt. John S. Wise observed: "The impression [which the man] made by his presence, and by his leadership, upon all who came in contact with him, can be described by no other term than that of grandeur." James Longstreet (right) was powerfully built and strongly opinionated, with a beard that concealed an unsmiling mouth. Some junior officers considered him deliberate; others thought him slow. Lee called Longstreet "my old war horse." Col. Moxley Sorrel wrote that the First Corps commander "was like a rock of steadiness when sometimes in battle the world seemed flying to pieces."

Confederate Sunset *(bottom)*

Fredericksburg, February 1863
CONFEDERATE SUNSET *(study, top, right)*

Lee and his two corps commanders reconnoitered often that winter so as to be alert to any movements of note by the Union army. This painting depicts the three generals at sunset in a pine clearing near the Rappahannock River.

These were the last days the three men would be together. The gruff Longstreet was ever-anxious for independent command because, as he noted to Confederate senator Louis Wigfall, he saw "opportunities for all kinds of moves to great advantage." Longstreet finally got permission in February 1863 to take two divisions on a foraging expedition in southeastern Virginia.

When the three men were in conversation, Jackson always deferred to Lee and gave less than full attention to Longstreet's wordy statements. A member of Jackson's staff observed that Jackson remained "very reserved, not particularly companionable, but always . . . affable and polite." Of Lee, Lt. John S. Wise commented: "He assumed no airs of superior authority. . . . His bearing was that of a friend having a common interest in a common venture with the person addressed." Richmond artillerist Hampden Chamberlayne was more impressed. He thought Lee "silent, inscrutable, strong, like a God, beside whom [other] Generals are pygmies."

"[Jackson] challenged comparison with the most extraordinary phenomena in the annals of military genius. . . . It was difficult to say what this man had not accomplished that had ever before been accomplished in history with equal means."

—Edward A. Pollard, *The Second Year of the War,* 1863

Brief Encounter

Middleburg, Virginia, February 1863

In the early evening a Confederate squadron rides into Middleburg, Virginia, and stops at the Beveridge House, an inn that dated back to the 1700s. Some of the troopers are checking equipment and weapons; others wait patiently to continue the night ride.

The central figure here is a young officer tipping his hat in salute to "a fair damsel" seated quietly in her sleigh. Whether this is a flirtatious gesture or a greeting of acquaintance is unknown.

For the couple, however, it is a momentary respite from the stern atmosphere of war.

Loneliness was ever-present among soldiers and civilians alike. To love and be loved was life's greatest blessing. William Corson of the 3rd Virginia Cavalry believed so. To his fiancée Jennie, he wrote: "When I think of embracing you as my wife, the thought is perfectly blissful. . . . I have nearly worn out the little curl you gave me. I take it out every day to gaze upon and kiss."

Wayside Farewell

Middletown, Virginia, February 3, 1863

Saying good-bye can be the saddest moment in war. Such a farewell occurred in February 1863, in front of the Wayside Inn at Middletown, Virginia, a village along the Valley Turnpike.

An officer is about to depart from his wife. Tears can no longer be held back nor can encouraging words mask despair. Whether they will ever see each other again is a thought neither can ignore. So they press closely against each other for the strength that comes from togetherness.

Levels of education had little to do with expressions of love. Arkansas surgeon Junius Bragg told his wife: "If it were not for you, I would have nothing—no object in the world worth living for. The hope of happiness yet to come, and you its source, is my hope, my anchor."

Pvt. William Stilwell of the 53rd Georgia spoke his feelings in poetry-prose. "I watch for thee when eve's first star shines dimly in the heavens afar, and twilight mists and shadows gray upon the lake's broad waters play. When not a breeze or sound is heard to startle evening's lonely bird but hushed is even the humming bee, then, dearest love, I watch for thee."

"If it were **not for you,** I would have **nothing**—no object in the world **worth living for.** The hope of happiness yet to come, and you its source, is **my hope, my anchor."**

—Asst. Surgeon Junius Bragg, 33rd Arkansas

Winter Riders

Raleigh, North Carolina,
February 5, 1863

Few Civil War paintings
portray life far behind the
front lines. One reason for
Mort Künstler's eminence as
a Civil War artist is his ability
to portray human nature and
drama far from a battlefield.
The war was present there too,
and the sight of soldiers
in the street produced
instinctive feelings of
admiration and security.

It is early February 1863,
in Raleigh, the capital of North
Carolina—the state that would
suffer the heaviest losses in
the war. A detachment of
cavalry rides down one of the
main boulevards at nightfall.
Behind them is the capitol
building. From its dome fly
the First National flag of the
Confederacy and the North
Carolina state banner. One of
the riders carries the Southern
battle flag recognizable
wherever Confederate troops
were present. Spectators silently
watch the procession.

"Everything quiet here in
N.C.," a matron in the eastern
region of the state wrote in her
journal at the time. Catherine
Edmondston's confidence
remained high. "I yield
nothing—no compromise—
where my liberty, my honour,
dearer than life, is concerned."

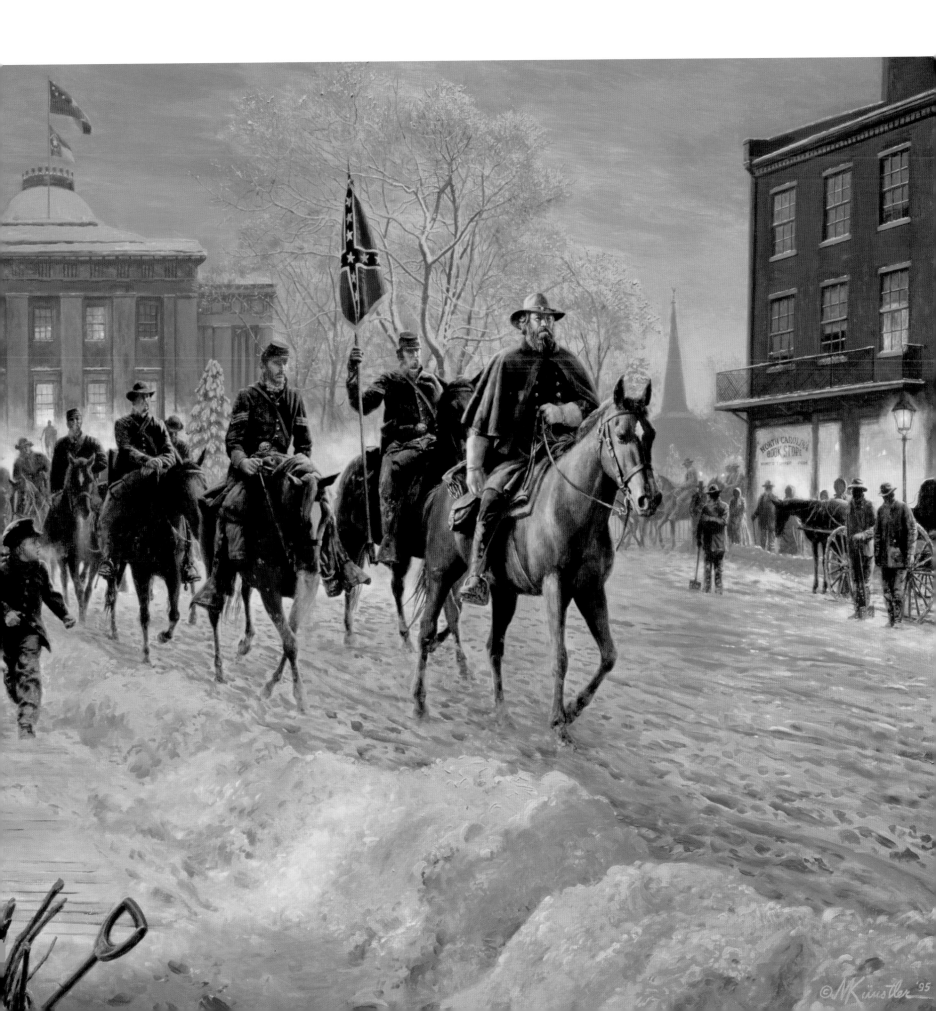

Bravest of the Brave

Black Horse Cavalry, Warrenton, Virginia, February 22, 1863 *(opposite)*

Organized in 1859 in Fauquier County, Virginia, the Black Horse Troop entered Confederate service as Company H, 4th Virginia Cavalry Regiment. "In many respects," one of its members boasted, "it was a remarkable body of men, composed as it was of handsome, strapping, debonair Virginians, admirably horsed and equipped."

The 4th Virginia was with Stuart on the famous "ride around McClellan" expedition (see pages 57–59). Thereafter, the Black Horse Troop received praise for its "many bold reconnaissances" in northern Virginia. Its "good state of discipline and efficiency" made it a model unit. In fact, the company's persistence in carrying out its duties in all kinds of weather, with little food and forage, and sometimes at great peril for its small number, led Virginians to call the troop "the bravest of the brave."

Here they are silently passing through Warrenton, home to most of the riders. In the background is the Fauquier County courthouse.

The Fairfax Raid

John S. Mosby, Fairfax Court, Virginia, March 9, 1863

They called him the Gray Ghost of the Confederacy, and he thrived on it.

John S. Mosby was colonel of the 43rd Battalion, Virginia Cavalry. Officially, his men were partisan rangers; unofficially, they were guerrillas who farmed by day and fought by night. Their leader was a small wisp of a man, always restless and void of fear.

Mosby's greatest feat came on the night of March 8, 1863. Responding to a Union insult that he was nothing but a horse thief, Mosby and a handful of irregulars sneaked into the Union-held town of Fairfax Court House. Mosby reportedly awakened Gen. Edwin Stoughton in the house he was staying at by whacking him on the behind and asking: "Did you ever hear of Mosby?"

"You've caught him!" the half-asleep Stoughton asked joyfully.

"No," Mosby replied, "but he has caught you."

The *New York Times* called the capture "utterly disgraceful."

Yet Lincoln saw humor in Mosby's escapade. The president said he did not mind losing a brigadier as much as the horses Mosby captured, "for I can make a much better Brigadier in five minutes, but the horses cost a hundred and twenty-five dollars apiece." Stoughton was exchanged two months later but received no further army command.

Divine Guidance

Stonewall Jackson, March 1863

Two days after Jackson resumed operations in the field, he learned that Janie Corbin had died of scarlet fever. Jackson burst into tears and began praying. The epic movie *Gods and Generals* (2003) has a poignant scene of Jackson grieving, while an aide voices puzzlement that the general could sob over the loss of a child while seeming indifferent to all the soldier-deaths he had seen in the war. Another staff officer observes quietly: "I think he is crying for them all."

" … and The Two Generals Were Brought to Tears"

Jackson and Lee, Fredericksburg, Spring 1863

The religious practices of Lee and Jackson were along different paths. Nevertheless, the faith of each man was indisputable. This was evident when the two generals attended a religious revival meeting in late winter at the Thomas Yerby estate, Belvoir, near Fredericksburg.

Rev. Beverly Tucker Lacy, Jackson's corps chaplain, conducted the service. A Prussian visitor to the army, Capt. Julius Scheibert, said of Lacy: "I can not forget the fervor and power of his sermons." That morning Lacy "described the homes from which the army had been drawn" with such emotion that both generals were brought to tears.

At Lee's death in 1870, a New York newspaper proclaimed that he "came nearer the ideal of a soldier and a Christian general than any man we can think of." Rev. Robert Stiles, who served in the Army of Northern Virginia, said of Jackson: "He came nearer putting God in God's place than any man we have ever known."

Julia

Stonewall Jackson and Family, Guiney's Station, April 20, 1863

Monday, April 20, 1863, was one of the happiest days in Jackson's life. His wife Anna and the infant daughter he had never seen arrived at Guiney's Station (called Guinea Station today) near the army encampments. Soldiers cheered wildly at the sight of "Old Jack" with his family.

A misty rain did nothing to dampen the general's joy, Anna Jackson recalled: "His face was sunshine and gladness; and, after greeting [me], it was a picture, indeed, to see his look of perfect delight and admiration as his eyes fell upon that baby! . . . He was afraid to take her in his arms, with his wet overcoat; but as we drove in [the] carriage . . . his face reflected all the happiness and delight that were in his heart."

Jackson's chaplain, Rev. Beverly T. Lacy, baptized the child three days later. She was christened Julia Laura in honor of Jackson's mother and sister. The visit of his wife and child lasted only nine days before Union movements across the river signaled a resumption of the war. As wife and daughter prepared to depart southward by train, Jackson sent a note, Anna Jackson recalled, "explaining why he could not leave his post, and invoking God's love and blessing upon us."

Grierson's Butternut Guerrillas

Newton Station, Mississippi, April 24, 1863

As a first stage in Grant's move on Vicksburg, 1,700 Union cavalry embarked on a diversionary raid southward through Mississippi. The horsemen were to destroy supply and communications lines and create confusion to keep the Vicksburg defenders off-balance.

Chosen to lead the expedition was an unlikely hero named Benjamin Grierson. The dark-haired, gangling Scotch-Irishman was a music teacher from Illinois with no formal military experience. At the age of eight, a kick from a skittish horse left his face permanently scarred and himself distrustful of the animals.

Starting on April 17, 1863, the long Union column fought skirmishes as it braved Mississippi rain, mud, and heat. Many troopers wore Confederate uniforms to deceive the citizenry. At Newton Station, 100 miles east of Vicksburg, Grierson's men captured one train and then pounced on another as they destroyed vital supplies en route to the Mississippi River fortress.

The saddle-sore horsemen, smelling of sweat and wood smoke, reached Baton Rouge in sixteen days. They had covered 600 miles, torn up 56 miles of railroad, inflicted 100 casualties, and captured 500 Confederates—all at a cost of 24 men. William T. Sherman, always short with praise, called Grierson's feat "one of the most brilliant cavalry exploits of the war."

The Last Council

Jackson, Lee, and Stuart at Chancellorsville, Virginia, May 1, 1863 · THE LAST COUNCIL *(study, below)*

Late in April 1863, in an effort to strike at Lee's rear, Union general Joseph Hooker marched the bulk of the Army of the Potomac through the jungle-like Wilderness region of Virginia. The Southern commander reacted by shifting most of his army toward a Wilderness crossroad known as Chancellorsville. A seemingly puzzled Hooker assumed a defensive position.

On the night of May 1, Jeb Stuart reported to Lee that Hooker's right flank was "in the air"—not anchored on any natural barrier. Lee the hunted now became Lee the hunter. "How do we get at those people?" he asked.

He studied his map and promptly answered his question. Jackson would take the larger part of the Southern army, make a sweeping march around the flank of the once-flanking Union army, and strike Hooker from the west while Lee approached from the south.

Lee and Jackson were going to risk the future of the Confederacy with an incredible gamble. Yet because Lee was so badly outnumbered, he could take enormous risks—such as attack a heavily armed force with the element of surprise rather than the presence of strength.

The Last Meeting

Chancellorsville, Virginia, May 2, 1863

Jackson was still wearing his raincoat when the head of his column began marching westward. Near 8 a.m. on May 2, the general rode forward with his staff. Lee was standing in a clearing of dead trees and old stumps. Jackson, face flushed and eyes blazing, reined his horse and spoke with the commander for several minutes.

James Power Smith of Jackson's staff remembered that the general's words were uttered quickly "as though all were distinctly formed in his mind and beyond all question."

Suddenly Jackson pointed to the west. Lee nodded. Then Jackson gave a quick salute, turned his horse, Little Sorrel, and rejoined his staff.

The two generals never saw each other again.

"... Cross Over the River"

General Thomas J. Jackson and Little Sorrel (right)

End of a Legend

Jackson, Chancellorsville, May 2, 1863 (below)

At 5 p.m. that Saturday, the thick woods suddenly exploded with gunfire and rebel yells. Jackson's two-mile-wide attack was a human wave that swept everything before it. One Union corps fell apart, the pieces trying futilely to stem the assault.

Nightfall three hours later found 30,000 men locked in combat. Hooker's line had bent back three miles, almost to the Chancellorsville crossroad. Jackson was not content. He decided that the attack must be continued into the night. The general himself rode forward with his staff to reconnoiter. On his return, Southern infantry mistook the riders for Union cavalry. A volley of gunfire came at point-blank range.

Three bullets struck Jackson. The damage from one led to amputation of his left arm. Lee responded to the news by writing

Jackson: "Could I have directed events, I should have chosen for the good of the country to have been disabled in your stead."

Jackson's condition slowly worsened. Eight days later, on the tenth—appropriately on the Sunday Sabbath—he murmured his last words: "Let us cross over the river and rest under the shade of the trees."

His Supreme Moment

Lee at Chancellorsville, May 3, 1863
HIS SUPREME MOMENT *(study, below)*

In the morning of the second day's battle at Chancellorsville, the two wings of the Confederate army reunited and drove the Federals northward through the Wilderness. The Chancellor house, Hooker's headquarters, was in flames as Lee emerged from the woods into the Chancellorsville clearing. Lee had won this battle against all odds. He knew it. His men realized it.

"The sight of the old hero after such a victory was too much," Georgia sergeant Micajah Martin told his parents. "We had never cheered him before, but now the pride we felt in him must have vent, and of all the cheering ever heard, this was our most enthusiastic."

Lee's aide, Col. Charles Marshall, was awestruck by the scene. Lee "sat in the full realization of all that soldiers dream of—triumph; and as I looked upon him in the complete fruition of the success which his genius, courage, and confidence in his army had won, I thought it must have been from such a scene that men in ancient days ascended to the dignity of gods."

"The sight of the old hero

after such a victory was too much. . . . the

pride we felt in him must have vent,

and of all the **cheering** ever heard, this

was our most enthusiastic."

—Sgt. Micajah Martin, 2nd Georgia

Going Home *(below)* · Last Tribute of Respect *(following pages)*

Stonewall Jackson Funeral Service, Virginia, May 12–15, 1863

Some 25,000 mourners passed by Jackson's coffin as it lay in state in the capitol rotunda at Richmond. A matron visiting the capital wrote: "I never saw human faces show such grief—almost despair." The city's largest newspaper proclaimed: "The affections of every household in the nation were twined around this great and unselfish warrior. . . . He has fallen, and a nation weeps."

A Massachusetts soldier spoke for the North when he made a simple observation: "We shall fear him no more."

A train bore the remains to Lynchburg on May 13. After a funeral cortege through town, the casket (wrapped in the new Third National Confederate flag) was placed aboard the canal boat *Marshall* (below). A large crowd, including 1,500 convalescent soldiers from local hospitals, watched the vessel slowly head upriver to Lexington and the final funeral service.

On May 14, Jackson's casket was brought to the Virginia Military Academy where it lay in state in his former classroom guarded by cadets. On the fifteenth, Stonewall Jackson was laid to rest in the Lexington cemetery that now bears his name.

"The **affections** of every household in the nation were **twined around this** great and unselfish **warrior.** ... He has fallen, and a nation weeps."

—*Richmond Dispatch*

Col. Robert Shaw and the 54th Massachusetts

Boston, May 28, 1863

The first all-volunteer black regiment formed in the North was the 54th Massachusetts. Freedmen and former slaves were virtually handpicked because the unit was to be a showcase, hopefully, for many others to follow. Robert Gould Shaw, son of a prominent Boston family, agreed to become colonel.

Although the recruits were well drilled and tightly disciplined, widespread doubt existed about their ability to fight on a level with white soldiers. The 54th Massachusetts dispelled such uncertainties on July 18, 1863, when it was part of a near-suicidal attack across the beach at Fort Wagner, South Carolina. Shaw and almost half of his troops died valiantly in the action.

The *Atlantic Monthly* proclaimed: "Through the cannon smoke of that dark night, the manhood of the colored race shines before many eyes that would not see."

More than 180,000 blacks ultimately served as Union soldiers. A third of them perished from battle and sickness.

"If all our people get their freedom, we can afford to die."

—Soldiers from the 54th Massachusetts

Before the Ball

Gen. J. E. B. Stuart, Culpeper, Virginia, June 4, 1863

Jeb Stuart, Lee's gregarious cavalry chief, loved music and a party. He spent the month following Chancellorsville in assembling, resting, and drilling his four mounted brigades. Stuart decided to stage a formal review on June 5 near his Culpeper headquarters; the night before, he stated, there would be a grand ball.

"Invitations were issued far and near," Capt. William Blackford stated, "and as the time approached every train came loaded with visitors." Carriages, wagons, and ambulances "distributed beauty at every hospitable gate," Maj. von Borcke

of Stuart's staff observed. The town hall underwent conversion to a ballroom. Near 8 p.m., officers in dress uniforms and ladies wearing the finest fashions the wartime South could provide began gathering.

A high moment in the preliminaries was the arrival of Stuart and his wife Flora. Near Stuart are Gens. Fitzhugh Lee and Wade Hampton. Aides Heros von Borcke and John Esten Cooke are behind them. Regimental flags from Virginia, North Carolina, South Carolina, and Georgia adorn the hall.

Candlelight and Roses

Stuart at the Culpeper Ball, June 4, 1863

Stuart's June 4 ball was the greatest extravaganza the town of Culpeper knew during the war. The flamboyant Stuart decorated the town hall with every adornment his men could find. One newspaper reporter thought it a "gay and dazzling scene, illuminated by a flood of light from numerous chandeliers." A romantic mood hung over the soiree.

Here, Stuart and his wife have entered the hall. Several dancing couples are unaware of their presence because the band continues to play. Among the dancers (left foreground) are Gen. Wade Hampton and an admirer. Looming over Stuart was his six-feet-four-inch Prussian aide, von Borcke. Cooke (a future biographer of Lee as well as Jackson) is behind von Borcke. In the right foreground, dancing with the lady in the green gown, is the commanding general's nephew, Gen. Fitzhugh Lee.

The ball lasted until midnight.

The Grand Review

Brandy Station, Virginia, June 5, 1863

Union cavalry had never been a real threat to Jeb Stuart up to this midway point of the war. He therefore took special delight—and little caution—in pulling all of his mounted units together for a grand review. The site was Brandy Station, a few miles north of Culpeper.

June 5 was bright and sunny. Crowds were at vantage points on ground overlooking a large plain. The review began in midmorning. Over 9,500 cavalrymen formed a line a mile and a half long. All cheered Stuart as he first rode up and down the ranks of his troopers.

Then the general took a position on a knoll to watch twenty-two mounted regiments dash by with swords brandishing. "The effect was thrilling," Capt. Blackford remembered. "The ladies clasped their hands and sank into the arms, sometimes, of their escorts in a swoon." Although artillerist James A. Williams thought the affair "a useless expenditure of powder and horse flesh," he also confessed that "it was one of the grandest scenes I ever saw."

That moment was the peak of Stuart's fame. Four days later, Union cavalry made a surprise attack at Brandy Station that caught Confederates totally off guard.

"**The men** were in splendid condition and **in high spirits.** As they passed through the village the soldiers closed up their ranks and the **bands played** as if on parade."

—Front Royal, Virginia, resident Thomas Ashby

Covered with Glory

26th North Carolina at Front Royal, Virginia, June 20, 1863

By mid-June, the two columns of Lee's army were marching north on either side of the Blue Ridge Mountains. It was a powerful force of 75,000 soldiers. They were ill-equipped and underfed, but fresh from a stunning victory at Chancellorsville, Johnny Rebs were confident about the results of this new campaign.

Among the outstanding regiments in A. P. Hill's corps was the veteran 26th North Carolina, the axis in Gen. Johnston Pettigrew's all-Tar Heel brigade.

On June 20, the Carolinians were in the long line of soldiers passing through Front Royal, Virginia. The entire population turned out to encourage the happy warriors. Resident Thomas Ashby wrote: "The men were in splendid condition and in high spirits. As they passed through the village the soldiers closed up their ranks and the bands played as if on parade."

The two mounted officers are Col. Henry K. Burgwyn Jr. and Lt. Col. John R. Lane. Three days earlier, the twenty-one-year-old Burgwyn had written his mother: "What will be the result of the movement now afoot God alone can tell."

Three of every four men in the 26th North Carolina, including their "boy colonel," would be killed or wounded in the next two weeks.

God Be with You

Lee and Longstreet, Berryville, Virginia,
June 21, 1863 (above)

The Confederate advance out of Virginia
was slow because of the need to forage
for food. Moreover, Lee was not well. His
health was precarious, and the past weeks
had been unusually stressful.

Lee reached the village of Berryville,
through which Longstreet's corps was
passing. Lee dismounted in front of the
courthouse. Refugee Judith McGuire had
earlier noted in her diary: "Berryville is a
little village surrounded by . . . delightful
society. Patriotism burns brightly there,
and every one is busy for the country in
his own way."

Since it was Sunday, June 21, the army
commander paused to attend morning
services at nearby Grace Episcopal
Church. As Lee prepared to remount
Traveler, undoubtedly one or more of the
townspeople bade him farewell with the
customary wish of that day: "God be
with you."

"Maryland, My Maryland"

26th North Carolina, Potomac Crossing, June 25, 1863 *(below)*

Certainly the most dramatic moment in both of Lee's expeditions into the North was crossing the Potomac River. The great stream was the geographical dividing line between North and South. Whoever passed over it was the aggressor.

Just after sunrise on June 25, Gen. Johnston Pettigrew's North Carolina soldiers waded through the river. The site was Boteler's Ford, near Shepherdstown. There the Potomac was 150 yards wide, with an uneven bottom, but the water was never more than waist-deep. Julius Hineback of the 26th North Carolina noted: "Taking off our shoes, socks, pants, and drawers we made a comical looking set of men."

Pettigrew (upper left) watched as his men splashed ashore. Some gave the rebel yell on reaching Yankee territory. Others, with the regimental band of the 26th North Carolina providing accompaniment, sang "Maryland, My Maryland," a poignant protest written in 1861 after Union troops occupied Baltimore.

CHAPTER FOUR

HIGH WATER MARK

LEE MADE THE DECISION TO STRIKE NORTH for both offensive and defensive reasons. A clear victory on Union soil might increase Northern war weariness to the point of letting the South have its independence. At the least, Lee could collect badly needed supplies from a heretofore undisturbed countryside. Lee confessed before the movement began: "The question of food for this army gives me more trouble and uneasiness than everything else combined."

An invasion into the North would also draw Hooker from Virginia; it would force Lincoln to think about the safety of Washington rather than the capture of Richmond. There was additionally the lingering hope that a spectacular success would prompt England and/or France to grant recognition and aid to the Confederacy.

To fill the void left by Jackson's death, Lee reorganized his army into three corps led by James Longstreet, Richard Ewell, and A. Powell Hill. The rebuilt Army of Northern Virginia routed Federals at Winchester, crossed the Potomac in June, and proceeded unmolested into Pennsylvania. Thirty-seven brigades, with 250 cannons and miles of wagons,

snaked through the peaceful farmland. Mixed reactions came from citizens. One stated: "Most of [Lee's] men were exceedingly dirty, some ragged, some without shoes, and some surrounded by the skeletons of what had once been an entire hat." Another thought Lee's men "well armed and under perfect discipline."

Optimism was high inside the ranks. Artillerist William Rouett wrote his cousin: "Would that our Enemys should feel the effects of war as we do, perhaps they would stop fighting." Lee felt confident. "The fact is," Gen. Henry Heth observed, "General Lee believed that the Army of Northern Virginia . . . could accomplish anything."

By June 28, Lee's forces were strung out in a forty-five-mile arc with Ewell's corps almost in sight of the state capital, Harrisburg. With his army attenuated in enemy territory, Lee was in no position to fight. The Union army supposedly was south of the Potomac, Lee assumed, because he had heard nothing from the reconnoitering Jeb Stuart.

The whole situation changed that night. A Confederate spy informed Lee that the Union army was at Frederick,

Maryland, on his flank and continuing to march. The Army of the Potomac was nearer to the fragments of Lee's army than the pieces were to one another. Equally bad, a new general headed the Union army: George G. Meade, a close friend of Lee's in the prewar army. Lee knew Meade as a solid fighter who did not make mistakes. Meade "will commit no blunder on my front," Lee told his officers, "and if I make one, he will make haste to take advantage of it." Lee issued immediate orders. The advance would halt; the three corps would reunite as quickly as possible somewhere in the area of a convenient road hub called Gettysburg.

Meanwhile, Meade had inherited an army with a shaky organization. In the past ten months, it had fought four major battles under a different commander. Not one of the seven army corps had the same commander as a year ago at Antietam. An unstable chain of command, however, seemed to toughen the troops, Capt. Stephen Weld of the 18th Massachusetts felt. They "have something of the English bull-dog in them. You can whip them time and again, but the next fight they go into, they are . . . as full of pluck as ever. . . . Some day or other we shall have our turn."

Meade moved his army north to keep his force between Lee and Baltimore. On June 30, he dispatched two cavalry brigades and six pieces of artillery to search for Lee's army. At the head of this reconnaissance in force was Gen. John Buford. On reaching Gettysburg, Buford immediately noted the strategic importance of the town and its nearby ridges. He posted his cavalry and sent word for Union infantry to hasten to Gettysburg.

Early on the morning of July 1, one of Powell Hill's Confederate divisions came marching from the west, lured by the report of a large number of shoes stored in the town. A spirited fight erupted between Northern cavalry and Southern infantry. Ewell's divisions arrived and attacked from the north. Even though Lee did not wish to bring on a general engagement until his whole army was at hand, the battle became general by human magnetism.

Violence was now occurring on two fronts, and the Federal line was being beaten into an L-shape. Lee arrived on the field in early afternoon. Longstreet's half of the army was still en route. Victory was close at hand. Lee thereupon changed his mind and ordered a general advance by both Hill and Ewell.

The Union lines broke. Confederates chased the disorganized pieces through town. Federals took cover on Cemetery Ridge. A final attack that Lee desperately wanted never materialized. At nightfall, segments of the Union army were moving steadily onto the high ground south of Gettysburg.

Casualties that day had been appalling. Over 9,000 of approximately 19,000 Federals engaged and 6,000 of some 25,000 Confederates had been killed, wounded, or captured. The famed Iron Brigade lost 1,200 of 1,800 men. The 26th North Carolina took 850 men into the fight and had 250 left at day's end. Young Robin Berkeley of a Virginia battery looked at the day's carnage: "It would have satiated the most blood-thirsty and cruel man on God's earth." Berkeley added: "Great God! When will this horrid war stop?"

It could not stop at that point. Both Lee and Meade were locked in combat, and they had to finish what had been so violently unleashed.

Sunrise, July 2, found the Union line resembling a fishhook, the barbed end starting at Culp's Hill, curving 180 degrees around Cemetery Ridge, and ending two miles away at Little Round Top. The anchored flanks, plus the convex shape of the line, made it easy to shift reinforcements quickly from one sector to another. In contrast, the Southern battle line was concave, nearly twice as long, with serious communication problems.

Still unsure of Federal strength, Lee ordered a two-pronged attack. Longstreet with the main force would assault the Union left flank. Ewell, at the sound of Longstreet's guns, would assail Meade's right. This strategy, Lee hoped, would crumble the Union flanks and break the position before all of the Federal army could get in place.

Nothing worked for Lee that day—starting with the fact that Meade's forces were already in position. With no word from his cavalry chief, Stuart, Lee was operating blind. Further, leading the main attack was Longstreet, the general most opposed to Lee's plan. The hoped-for early assault did not get under way until 4 p.m.

The second day's battle began with confusion on both sides. On the Union left was the corps of Gen. Daniel Sickles, a New York politician with personal ambitions. Bothered by

Rush to the Summit (study), Little Round Top, July 2, 1863

the low ground at the south end of Cemetery Ridge, Sickles on his own initiative moved two divisions to higher ground along a road stretching southwest from Gettysburg. There the Union soldiers held a salient with its apex in a peach orchard and its left situated in an area of boulders and stunted trees known as Devil's Den.

This unauthorized move left Little Round Top unprotected and both of Sickles' flanks vulnerable to attack. It also altered the direction of Longstreet's attack after it began and entirely changed the course of the battle.

For hours vicious fighting raged amid rocks, fields, and woody hillsides. Lines of soldiers swayed back and forth in combat; artillery fire mixed with heavy musketry added to the chaos of hand-to-hand struggles. One Confederate assault at Little Round Top almost got in the rear of Meade's army, but a gallant stand by Lawrence Chamberlain's 20th Maine kept the line intact.

©MKünstler '93

"Naught could be heard but the hoarse **roar** of the cannon, the **screaming** and **bursting** of shells … the unearthly **cries** of wounded horses."

—Capt. William J. Seymour, 6th Louisiana

On the opposite end of the Union position, Ewell's men attacked belatedly and disjointedly. What gains they made, they lost by day's end.

Some of the bloodiest fighting of the war occurred that day. Yet the story was the same for the Confederates. Weary from delays and sapped by heat and lack of water, Lee's men fought aggressively at first but simply could not find the strength or coordination to exploit any advantage. Union losses were another 9,000 men; Lee suffered 6,500 casualties.

Lee's decision for July 3 was to attack again. He had gained ground in both days' actions. To retire now would be shattering to his soldiers' morale. Moreover, withdrawing in the face of an undefeated enemy would be complicated and dangerous. Above all considerations were Lee's audacious nature and his belief in the invincibility of his army.

Convinced that Meade had weakened his center to strengthen his flanks, Lee ordered an extensive bombardment of that sector, to be followed by a massive infantry attack. At 1 p.m. that intensely hot day, the greatest bombardment in the history of the hemisphere began. Confederate cannons along a two-mile front roared without interruption. Virginia soldier William Old wrote: "The hole Earth Seem to Be in a perfect Motion." Capt. William J. Seymour of the 6th Louisiana recalled that "Naught could be heard but the hoarse roar of the cannon, the screaming and bursting of shells . . . the unearthly cries of wounded horses." A Federal private

was more descriptive: "It was the most terrible scene and made one truly believe 'Hell was empty, and all the devils were there.'"

The cannonade ceased between 1 and 2 p.m., the smoke lifted, and there—at wood's edge and in plain view of Union soldiers—stood eleven brigades of Southern infantry. They were in battle array, with flags flying and bayonets shining. It looked like the start of a grand parade. Confederate Gen. Alexander Wright thought otherwise. "The real difference," he said, "is to stay there after you get there, for the whole infernal Yankee army is up there in a bunch."

"It was the most terrible scene and made one truly believe **'Hell was empty, and all the devils were there.'"**

—a Federal private

To the Wall

Battle alignment was by divisions. Johnston Pettigrew's men were on the left, George Pickett's division on the right, with Isaac Trimble's small force in support. When the Southerners started forward across that mile-wide plain, they gave an irresistible appearance. Yet the planning behind the attack was makeshift. Pettigrew, who had never commanded a brigade, led one that had already lost half its strength in the first day's fighting. Pickett's men were untested, and Trimble had taken command of his division just hours before the attack.

Directly in front of them was the II Corps: 9,000 of the best soldiers the Union army had, with a hard-fighting commander, Winfield Scott Hancock. Covering their flanks were 100 carefully positioned cannons.

Pickett's men made contact first. Hancock swung a brigade out to deliver a flanking fire in conjunction with artillery. The enfilade shredded the Southern column. "We could

not help hitting them at every shot," one gunner declared. Maj. Charles Peyton of the 19th Virginia recalled that Union cannons fired "with fearful effect, sometimes as many as ten men being killed and wounded by the bursting of a single shell."

The attack by Pettigrew ran into a sheet of musket fire in front and artillery blasts on the flank. "Arms, heads, blankets, guns, and knapsacks were thrown and tossed into the clear air," a Union officer stated. "A moan went up from the field, distinctly to be heard amid the storm of battle."

Gunfire was deafening; smoke blocked vision. Confederates were giving their battle screams, while Union soldiers shouted "Fredericksburg! Fredericksburg!" with the same vengeful feeling of Texans a quarter-century ago yelling "Remember the Alamo!" Living men trampled over the dead, while from injured soldiers came calls for help that no one heard.

Suddenly it was all over. First singly and then in groups, Confederates began staggering back across that terrible field to the woods far away. Hancock's corps had suffered more than 1,500 losses in repelling the attack. Some Union officers sought without success to get their benumbed soldiers to give pursuit. Both sides had done all they could. When Meade saw the Confederates drifting away from Cemetery Ridge, he grabbed his hat as if to swing it in joy, thought better of it, and quietly said: "Thank God."

Half of the nearly 14,000 soldiers in "Pickett's Charge" were killed, wounded, or captured. Only one field officer escaped injury. Twenty-eight regimental flags were captured. William H. Cocke of Lewis Armistead's brigade mourned the passing of so many of his closest friends. "I feel perfectly lost," he wrote home.

Casualties in the three days at Gettysburg exceeded 51,000 men. Lee lost a third of his men. The next day he issued orders by which the army would find its way back to the Potomac crossing. The retreat began in driving rain.

A Confederate officer wrote contemptuously that Meade "pursued us as a mule goes on the chase of a grizzly bear—as if catching up with us was the last thing he wanted to do." In reality, Meade had lost a fourth of the Army of the Potomac in the battle. He was understandably cautious in giving chase.

Lee's forces returned to Virginia disappointed but defiant. The 33rd North Carolina's James Weston put it succinctly: "We failed only because it was impossible to succeed."

"We failed only because it was impossible to succeed."

—Maj. James Weston,
33rd North Carolina

Lee on Traveler

"Oh, I Wish He Was Ours!"

Gen. Lee, Hagerstown, Maryland, June 26, 1863 *(opposite)*

On June 26, as Lee was accompanying his troops from Hagerstown, Maryland, to Chambersburg, Pennsylvania, a group of ladies suddenly surrounded him. One asked for a lock of his hair. Lee parried the request by pointing to his rapidly thinning hair. He referred the souvenir hunters to Gen. George Pickett, whose ringlets fell to his shoulders.

Farther up the road, with Lee lost in thought, a Northern girl was waving a Union flag at the column. "Oh," she blurted out as Lee rode past, "I wish he was ours!"

Lee's chief of staff, Col. Walter Taylor, was following the commander on horseback. If Taylor overheard the remark, he kept it to himself.

The Road to Gettysburg *(below)*

Most of Lee's men were lean and mean when they entered Pennsylvania. It was the undisputed land of the enemy. Strict orders existed against looting, but soldiers were desperate for food, shoes, and hats. They got them. "The prices have been to us Dixie boys remarkably moderate," the 27th Virginia's Watkins Kearns noted sarcastically.

A company-level officer gave a partial explanation for much of the looting. "It is rather a hard matter to restrain our troops when they remember the devastated plains of Virginia and the conduct of the Federals in other portions of our country."

One Pennsylvania woman, with a miniature Union flag adorning her blouse, stared contemptuously at the passing Confederate column until a Texas soldier sent her scurrying to cover with the announcement: "Take care, madam, for Hood's boys are great at storming breastworks when the Yankee colors is on them!"

Rendezvous with Destiny

Gen. John Buford, Gettysburg, June 30, 1863

Gen. John Buford was a little-publicized but highly capable cavalry officer commanding two brigades of New York and Illinois horsemen. Like Lincoln, Buford had been born in Kentucky and raised in Illinois. He was unassuming, but a hard-riding former Indian fighter. One trooper called Buford "a model commander"; another thought him "the best cavalry officer produced on this continent." Whether he was all of that was not as important as the fact that his soldiers believed it.

Miles ahead of the Union army, Buford was under orders to "cover and protect the front, and communicate all information of the enemy rapidly and surely." At 11 a.m. on June 30, Buford's men galloped into Gettysburg and past the Adams County courthouse. Residents greeted the Union troopers with cheering and needed food. It was apparent at once to Buford that converging roads and the lay of the land made Gettysburg as good a battleground as the Federals were likely to find.

Eve of Battle

Gen. John Buford, Gettysburg, June 30, 1863 *(opposite, top)*

John Buford was one of those plain-as-an-old-shoe soldiers who became conspicuous in the Civil War. Theodore Lyman of Meade's staff described him as "a compactly built man of middle height, with a tawny mustache and a little, triangular gray eye, whose expression is determined, not to say sinister. His ancient corduroys are tucked into a pair of cowhide boots and his blue blouse is ornamented with holes; from one pocket thereof peeps a huge pipe, while the other is fat with a tobacco pouch."

On the night of June 30, Buford paced back and forth on the Lutheran Theological Seminary grounds—just north of the eponymous Seminary Ridge (see page 150)—as he pondered what the Confederates would do the next day. His men were "fagged out," low on food and forage, with too many mounts in need of shoeing. Buford told one of his subordinates: "They will attack you in the morning, and they will come booming—skirmishers three deep. You will have to fight like the devil until support arrives!"

Morning Riders

Gen. Buford and Staff, Gettysburg, July 1, 1863, 5:15 AM *(below)*

All alone, at the head of an undersized cavalry division—with the Confederate army somewhere just beyond the western ridges and the Army of the Potomac strung out for miles behind him—John Buford wrestled with anxiety throughout the night of June 30–July 1. At dawn he mounted his horse and began reviewing his thin lines. The staff knew him as a man dedicated to his work and intolerant of nonchalance.

Word came at sunrise that John F. Reynolds' I Corps was close to Gettysburg, with Oliver O. Howard's XI Corps not too far behind. Buford's spirits rose. Teenage civilian Daniel Skelly wrote that the general's "calm demeanor and soldierly appearance . . . struck me forcibly."

Buford later wrote: "I had gained positive information of the enemy's position and movements, and my arrangements were made for entertaining him until General Reynolds could reach the scene."

"There's the Devil to Pay!"

Gens. John Buford and John F. Reynolds, Gettysburg, June 30, 1863 *(below)*

By 10 a.m. Buford's line on McPherson's Ridge, a mile west of Gettysburg, seemed about to snap. Up rode Gen. Reynolds. His I Corps was double-timing onto the field.

Reynolds looked down at the dismounted Buford and inquired lightly: "What's the matter, John?"

"There's the devil to pay!" Buford replied, pointing toward the lines of assaulting Southerners.

Reynolds then declared: "I hope you can hold out until my corps comes up."

In his typical laconic way, Buford answered: "I reckon I can."

The action now escalated into the largest battle of the war. Buford later reported: "A heavy task was before us, and we were equal to it, and shall remember with pride that at Gettysburg we did our country much service."

Five months later, John Buford died of typhoid fever.

"Hold at All Cost!"

Gen. Buford's Cavalry, Gettysburg, July 1, 1863, 9:30 AM *(opposite, top)*

Buford dismounted three-fourths of his troopers (the others held horses to the rear) and placed the men in a long and dangerously thin line on the ridges west and north of town. Each man was three feet from the next. The Federals took position behind fences and man-made works. Their one advantage was in being armed with single-shot breech-loading rifles that fired faster than the standard musket.

Gunfire began at 7:30 a.m on July 1. Soon Confederates were advancing in a mile-wide line. Buford's 2,500 horsemen were facing 7,000 enemy soldiers. For two hours the countryside echoed from battle. Buford's bloodied ranks began to sag under the weight of the relentless Confederate attack.

General Reynolds and Staff

Gettysburg, July 1, 1863

John Reynolds could have been commander of the Army of the Potomac, but a month before Gettysburg he declined the offer for the McClellan-like reason that Washington would not give him a "free hand" in decision-making.

Reynolds was then forty-two, "regular army" to the core, and an officer as respected as he was admired. He had made his I Corps into a hard-hitting unit that would be virtually destroyed at Gettysburg.

When Meade learned of the fighting on the morning of July 1, he exclaimed: "Good God! If the enemy get Gettysburg, we are lost!" Reynolds reassured the commander that his corps would fight "inch by inch" to defend the town.

Reynolds had just launched his own assault with the cry "Forward! For God's sake, forward!" when a sharpshooter killed him with a bullet behind the right ear.

"A heavy task was before us, and we were equal to it, and shall remember with pride that at Gettysburg we did our country much service."

—Gen. John Buford

"I cannot think of

what has become

of Stuart; I ought to

have heard from him long

before now."

—Gen. Robert E. Lee

"Strike Up a Lively Air" *(study, opposite, top)* · Distant Thunder *(opposite, bottom)*

Cashtown, Pennsylvania, July 1, 1863

Here is an instance where one addition changes the entire complexity of a painting.

In the first rendition, a column of infantry with a regimental band is passing through the village of Cashtown, eight miles from Gettysburg. A recent shower has washed away the dust; the day is warm, the men well fed by bountiful Pennsylvania crops.

Insert a mounted Lee into the foreground and the mood changes abruptly. It is still July 1, but Lee is riding toward the distant thunder of battle. "I cannot think of what has become of Stuart," he says of his cavalry chief. "I ought to have heard from him long before now."

Lee rode east like a blinded giant. He was unfamiliar with the country. How much of his army was engaged in the action ahead? Was Meade's entire force on the field? Was Lee riding toward a grand opportunity or a great calamity? Never in his military career had Lee been so dangerously in the dark.

Hubert Dilger at Gettysburg

July 1, 1863 *(above)*

One of the dramatic moments in the first day's fighting came as Confederates slowly drove the XI Corps southward. That is when they encountered "Leatherbreeches."

Hubert Dilger was a former army officer in the Grand Duchy of Baden, part of the German Confederation. He emigrated to America and became captain of a battery in the 1st Ohio Artillery. Scientific as a gunner, fearless as an officer, Dilger was called "Leatherbreeches" because of the doeskin trousers he liked to wear.

Lacking orders or precedence, the handsome, well-mustached Dilger called for two of his guns to advance without infantry support to the aid of retreating Federals. His other two artillery pieces (shown here in the background on the right) continued firing.

Union cannoneer Augustus Buell gave a kaleidoscopic word-picture of the action that day: "Up and down the line, men reeling and falling; splinters flying from wheels and axles where bullets hit; in the rear, horses tearing and plunging, mad with wounds or terror; drivers yelling, shells bursting, shot shrieking overhead, howling about our ears or throwing up great clouds of dust where they struck; the musketry crashing on three sides of us; bullets hissing, humming and whistling everywhere. . . . Smoke, dust, splinters, blood, wreck and carnage indescribable."

"Are You Hurt, Sir?"

Gens. John B. Gordon and Richard Ewell, Gettysburg, July 1, 1863 *(above)*

A first-rate division commander with a quirky personality, Richard Ewell had lost a leg eleven months earlier at Antietam and had recently returned to duty as commander of Jackson's old corps. Having to acclimate to both a peg leg and corps command impaired Ewell's performance at Gettysburg. Yet there was a light moment in the first day's fighting.

Ewell and his best brigadier, John B. Gordon of Georgia, were riding into the town square late in the day when Federal snipers fired at the generals. Gordon heard the thud of a bullet as it struck Ewell.

"Are you hurt, sir?" he inquired anxiously.

"No, no," a nonchalant Ewell replied. "But suppose that ball had struck you. We would have had the trouble of carrying you off the field, sir. You see how much better fixed I am for fight than you are. It don't hurt a bit to be shot in a wooden leg."

Chamberlain and the 20th Maine

Marching to Gettysburg, July 1, 1863 *(opposite)*

Throughout July 1, the 20th Maine with the V Corps was marching toward the sound of combat. Lawrence Chamberlain had been promoted to regimental colonel six weeks earlier.

It was shortly after noon that humid Tuesday when the regiment passed out of Maryland. Pvt. William Livermore recalled: "We unfurled our colors and gave three cheers for Pennsylvania." A warm reception awaited the men. "The people appear delighted to see us," William Lamson wrote his father. "They were out all along the road with water and milk for us."

Welcoming cheers continued as the blue column marched on into the night. To the west the men could hear "disturbances of the atmosphere, as though someone was beating a rug far over the horizon."

The day's twenty-six-mile march ended at midnight with a brief halt. By sunrise, the 20th Maine was marching rapidly to Gettysburg.

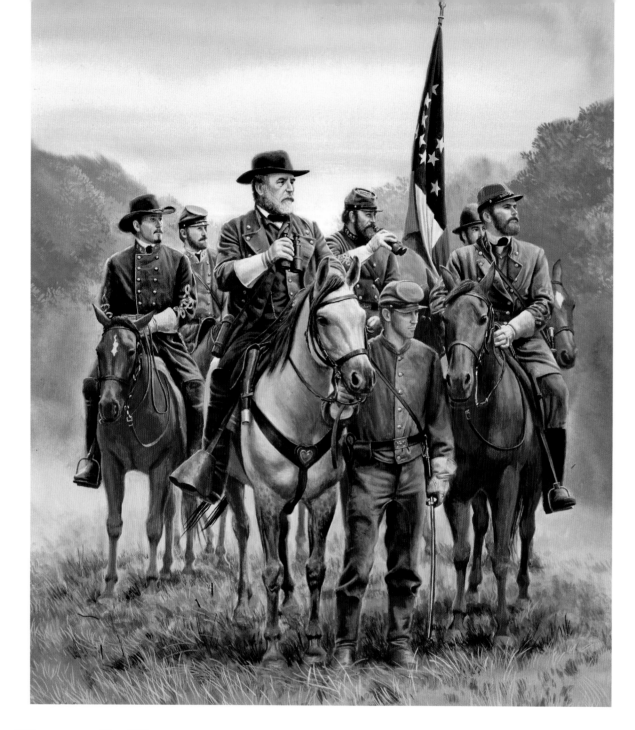

The Enemy Is There

Gen. Lee and Staff, Seminary Ridge, Gettysburg, July 1, 1863

As the final hours of July 1 passed, Lee faced mental decisions as well as physical problems. He had clearly won the smashing success on Northern soil he had wanted. Yet if he now retired from the field, a regrouped and pursuing enemy could strike him repeatedly on the march back to Virginia. Nor could Lee stand at Gettysburg and await the next Federal move. He did not have the ammunition, supplies, and food for a prolonged defensive stand. By elimination, his choice was to hammer the Union forces again before their whole army could concentrate. Lee made this decision without knowing Union strength. Stuart and his cavalry were still missing.

"If the enemy is there tomorrow," Lee said to his generals, "we must attack him."

This statement could not have been made with vitality. A heart attack in March still limited the general's activities. In addition, he had contracted "soldier's disease"—diarrhea—which was further sapping his effectiveness.

Twilight in Gettysburg

Gen. Lee, Gettysburg, July 1, 1863

The sun was setting on a vast, body-laden battlefield when Lee rode into the town square of Gettysburg. He had won a clear victory in the first day's fighting. Federals had been driven through town to high ground to the south. It was too late in the day for a continuation of the action. "Our people are not yet up," Lee observed, "and I have no troops with which to occupy this higher ground."

As Lee contemplated what to do, the loud cheers of soldiers around him interrupted his thoughts. The general removed his hat and acknowledged the praise. Lee's stern expression, however, revealed his disappointment that the day's action had not sent the Union army in full retreat.

The Grandest Charge Ever Seen

Barksdale's Mississippians, Gettysburg, July 2, 1863

William Barksdale looked more like an elder statesman than an impetuous general. Actually, he was both. A former newspaper editor, congressman, and outspoken secessionist, Barksdale had become the inspiring commander of what became known as Barksdale's Mississippi Brigade.

Throughout the afternoon of July 2, he chafed with impatience to put his troops into battle. Near 6 p.m., staff officer G. B. Lamar brought orders for Barksdale to advance. The general's face "was radiant with joy," Lamar stated. "He was in front of his brigade, his hat off, and his long white hair reminded me of the white plume of Navarre. I saw him as far as the eye could follow, still ahead of his men."

In what has been called "the grandest charge ever seen by mortal man," the Mississippians drove six hundred yards through the peach orchard. The Union line then stiffened. "Brave Mississippians!" Barksdale yelled. "One more charge and the day is ours!"

Fresh Union troops and concentrated artillery fire ripped the Southern ranks to pieces. Barksdale went down, shot in the chest and leg. Just before he died, he gasped to a Union surgeon: "Tell my wife I am shot, but we fought like hell!"

Hand to Hand

Little Round Top, July 2, 1863 *(above)*

What had once been a tranquil peach orchard became an arena for one of the bloodiest free-for-alls in the war. Men fought with savage desperation, giving ground only when driven to the ground.

Georgia brigadier Ambrose Wright described part of the action to his wife: "We must face . . . the network of bristling bayonets, which stretched around us on every side. . . . We rushed upon the flanking column [of the enemy] and literally cut our way out."

The 1st Minnesota went into the fight with 262 men. By nightfall, only forty-seven were left, and the unit took pride that there was not a straggler or prisoner on the casualty list.

Even the gruff Longstreet termed the action "the best three hours' fighting by any troops on any battlefield."

Rush to the Summit

Little Round Top, July 2, 1863 *(below)*

Meade's chief engineer, Gen. G. K. Warren, was making a last-minute inspection of the Union lines near noon on July 2 when he discovered Gen. Daniel Sickles's corps out of position and the Union left totally exposed. Warren's frantic call for help coincided with the arrival on the field of the lead brigades of the V Corps.

Col. Strong Vincent, a young Harvard graduate, led one of those brigades. It contained the 20th Maine, 16th Michigan, 44th New York, and 83rd Pennsylvania. Without waiting for any directive, Vincent ordered his men to occupy Little Round Top immediately.

Col. Chamberlain led the 20th Maine to the summit.

"Every soldier seemed to understand the situation, and to be inspired by the danger," Theodore Gerrish of the Maine regiment wrote. "Away we went, under the terrible artillery fire. . . . Up the steep hillside we ran." Little Round Top had to be secured, Capt. Eugene Nash of the 44th New York exclaimed. The empty height was "the key to the battlefield."

Hero of Little Round Top

Col. Joshua Chamberlain, Little Round Top, July 2, 1863

Col. Vincent deployed his brigade halfway up Little Round Top in an arc facing south and west. The 20th Maine was on the far flank. "This is the left of the Union line! You understand!" Vincent shouted to Col. Chamberlain. "You are to hold this ground at all costs!"

The 358 Maine soldiers took their position. Capt. Amos Judson of the 83rd Pennsylvania stated, "Scarcely had the troops been put in line when a loud, fierce, distant yell was heard, as if pandemonium had broken loose." A powerful flanking column came at Chamberlain's thin line.

Over a ninety-minute period, Confederates assaulted the Maine regiment's position five times. The Union line swayed and staggered from the attacks, but held firm. Amid reeking smoke, Chamberlain watched the action vacillate "with wild whirlpools and eddies. At times I saw around me more of the enemy than of my own men, gaps opening, swallowing, closing again."

By 7 p.m. a third of Chamberlain's regiment had fallen. The rest were running out of ammunition and preparing to swing their muskets as clubs when the next assault came. Perhaps because of his professorial background, Chamberlain was quick-witted. He later wrote: "Desperate as the chances were, there was nothing for it, but to take the offensive." He thereupon shouted: "Bayonets!"

Chamberlain's Charge

Little Round Top, July 2, 1863
CHAMBERLAIN'S CHARGE (study, below)

Possibly the charge worked because it was so unexpected.
One reason it did succeed was the condition of the
enemy. The Alabamians of Col. William C. Oates had
marched twenty-eight miles since 3 a.m., scrambled
uphill over rocks and through brush, encountered stiff
resistance in five separate attacks—all without a drop
of water. No energy was left in the living. "My dead
and wounded," Oates reported, "were then nearly as
great in number as those still on duty. . . . The blood
stood in puddles in some places on the rocks."

The 20th Maine's bayonet attack sent Confederates
reeling in confusion. Chamberlain remembered one
Southern officer firing a revolver with one hand while
he held out his sword in token surrender with the
other. "When the signal [for retreat] was given," Oates
admitted, "we ran like a herd of wild cattle." Over four
hundred Confederates laid down their arms as jubilant
Federals shouted: "On to Richmond!"

Years after the war, Oates reflected: "There never
were harder fighters than the Twentieth Maine and
their gallant Colonel. His skill and persistence and the
great bravery of his men saved Little Round Top and
the Army of the Potomac from defeat. Great events
sometimes turn on comparatively small affairs."

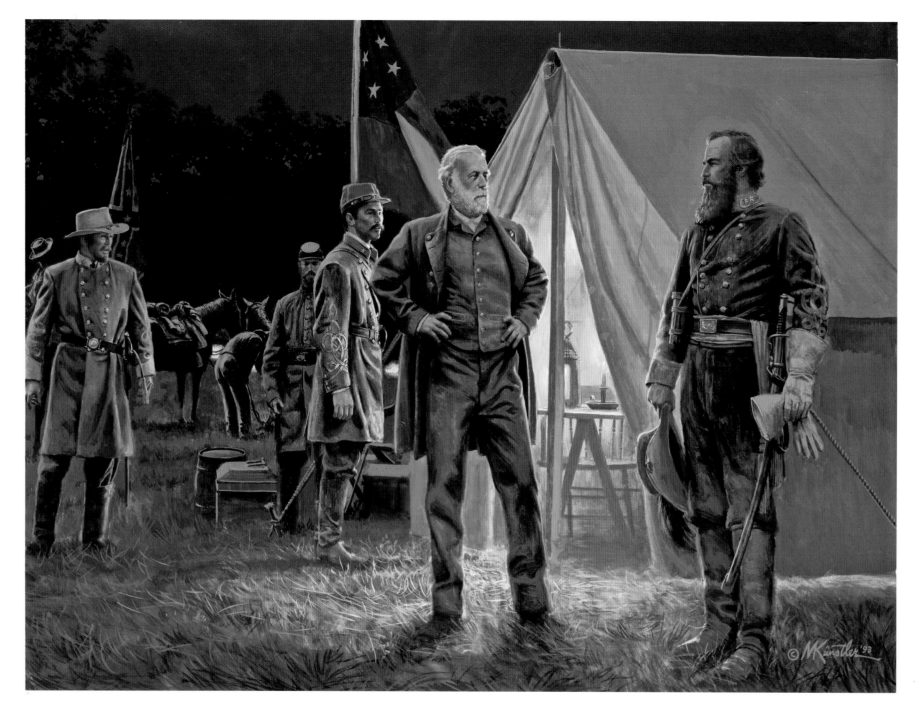

The Return of Stuart

Gens. Lee and Stuart, Gettysburg, July 2, 1863

No one questions the fact that Jeb Stuart's absence severely hampered Lee's thinking and actions during the Gettysburg campaign. As chief of cavalry, Stuart was the eyes of the army. The reconnaissance Lee so badly needed in enemy territory never materialized. "Without Stuart," Gen. Henry Heth stated, "the army was like a blindfolded giant."

Stuart veered from screening Lee's initial movements north, deciding instead to "pass around the rear of the Federal Army with three brigades and cross the Potomac between it and Washington" to confuse the enemy and collect supplies. Lee's orders to Stuart were indeed discretionary, but Stuart was not discreet in abandoning Lee after Confederates crossed the Potomac.

Just before sunset on July 2, Stuart arrived at Lee's headquarters. On rare occasions when Lee was displeased, his voice assumed an unmistakable, glacial tone. Tradition has it that Lee acknowledged Stuart's presence with the statement: "Well, General Stuart, you are here at last." In his official report, Lee's displeasure was clear: "The movements of the army preceding the battle of Gettysburg had been much embarrassed by the absence of cavalry."

Forming the Line

Col. Alexander and Gen. Longstreet, Gettysburg, July 3, 1863

A key actor in the July 3 drama was E. Porter Alexander, who has been called "probably the most brilliant and talented young officer in the Confederate army" at that time. His energy, confidence, and flexible intelligence had earned him a more varied career in six years out of West Point than many competent soldiers achieve in a lifetime.

In 1861 the impressive-looking Georgian had introduced the "wig-wag" method of signaling in warfare—a code system incorporating flag or torch motions that had been invented in the 1850s by U.S. Army surgeon Maj. Albert Myer, whom Alexander had once assisted. By the time of Gettysburg, Alexander was in tactical command of the artillery in Longstreet's corps. To him fell the responsibility of the bombardment that would soften the Union lines prior to the infantry attack. Alexander had batteries from all three corps—more than 150 guns—in place early that morning.

The hour-long cannonade began shortly after 1 p.m. Alexander wrote: "It was, indeed, a grand & exciting moment to hear our long line of guns break loose as if impatient of their long restraint & roaring in the very joy of battle." He felt cheerful and sanguine. "The fact is that like all the rest of the army, I believed that it would all come out right, because Gen. Lee had planned it."

The Guns of Gettysburg

Gettysburg, July 3, 1863

Artillery played a key role in every Civil War battle. Gettysburg was certainly no exception. The July 3 pre-attack bombardment by some 150 cannons produced what has been called "the loudest noise ever heard on the American continent." Although many of the shots went high, Sgt. John Plummer of the 1st Minnesota asserted: "It seemed that nothing four feet from the ground could live." Elisha Rhodes of the 2nd Rhode Island wrote: "Solid shot would strike the large rocks and split them as if exploded by gunpowder. The flying iron and pieces of stone struck men down in every direction."

Federal artillery fired 1,600 rounds just at Pettigrew's division as it entered the July 3 assault. Inside the town, a young citizen observed: "The vibrations could be felt, and the atmosphere was so full of smoke that one could taste the saltpeter."

Lee's "Old War Horse"

Longstreet and Lee, Gettysburg, July 3, 1863 *(opposite, top)*

What Gen. James Longstreet did—or did not do—at Gettysburg is an ongoing controversy that generates more heat than light. Confederate leaders said little at the time—and wrote much afterward. Observations and hindsight became hopelessly garbled.

Longstreet was the senior corps commander and anchor of Lee's army. His defenders assert that such status entitled him to argue strongly against Lee's battle strategies for July 2 and 3. "Old Pete," as he was nicknamed, was "never far from General Lee, who relies very much upon his judgment," British observer Col. Arthur Fremantle wrote. Through the campaign, Longstreet "was impatient to press forward" and "combative to the end."

To critics who claim that against Lee's orders Longstreet waited too long to attack during the morning of the second, Longsteet was a poor subordinate "who sulked because his plan was rejected by his chief" and accordingly "dragged his feet." Gen. John B. Gordon, one of Lee's most trusted generals, was the bluntest of all: Lee "died believing . . . that he lost Gettysburg at last by Longstreet's disobedience."

Famed twentieth-century historian Douglas Southall Freeman may have rendered the most judicious appraisal: "He should have obeyed orders, but the orders should not have been given."

Pickett's Salute

Gen. George E. Pickett, Gettysburg, July 3, 1863 *(right)*

Little about George E. Pickett was ordinary. Graduating last in his class at West Point in 1846, his military record was amazingly shallow until Longstreet took a liking to him. Pickett's rise to major general was meteoric.

Dandified in dress, effervescent in manner, Pickett was known more for his appearance than almost anything else. G. Moxley Sorrel of Longstreet's staff noted: "Long ringlets flowed loosely over his shoulders, trimmed and perfectly perfumed. His beard likewise was curling, and giving out the scents of Araby."

By the time of Gettysburg, the thirty-eight-year-old widower was hopelessly in love with a girl less than half his age. He had never enjoyed a big moment in the war, and he was about to get

it now. When Pickett asked Longstreet for permission to advance his division and the corps commander nodded silently, Pickett saluted smartly. "I am going to move forward, sir," he said, cheerfully composed and confident of success.

"Keep to Your Sabers, Men!"

Gens. George A. Custer and Wade Hampton, Gettysburg, July 3, 1863 (*previous pages*)

At almost the same time on July 3 that Confederates were assaulting Cemetery Ridge, Jeb Stuart was leading his own version of "Pickett's Charge." Lee had dispatched Stuart's cavalry to the extreme left to get behind the Union line and do damage. In midafternoon, Stuart's 3,000 horsemen charged 3,250 Federal cavalry under Gens. John Gregg and George A. Custer. "A grander spectacle than their advance has rarely been beheld," Capt. William Miller of the 3rd Pennsylvania Cavalry asserted. "Shell and shrapnel met the advancing Confederates and tore through their ranks. Closing the gaps as if nothing had happened, on they came."

All at once, Miller continued, "a crash, like the falling of timber, betokened the crisis. So sudden and violent was the collision that many of the horses were turned end over end and crushed their riders beneath them. The clashing of sabers, the firing of pistols . . . and cries of the combatants filled the air."

Union cavalry soon slammed into Stuart's flanks and broke the formation. Gen. Wade Hampton had just shouted "Keep to your sabers, men! Keep to your sabers!" when he went down temporarily with a scalp wound. Stuart withdrew. William Blackford of his staff called the fight "about as bloody and hot an affair as any we had yet experienced." Gen. Custer immodestly wrote of the final Union attack: "I challenge the annals of war to produce a more brilliant charge."

Men of Valor

Gettysburg, July 3, 1863 (*below*)

Just before the Confederate army headed north to Pennsylvania, William Winston of the 11th Virginia wrote his aunt: "Everything seems to indicate a bloody time. I have no doubt but that we will be successful but it will cost a great many lives."

Now the Johnny Rebs stood in line for the worst attack they had ever made. They had marched great distances on scant rations. Ill-clothed and at times shoeless, they had achieved valor amid incredible resilience. They were fighting for home, for constitutional rights as they interpreted them, and for honor.

"I never was scared as bad in my life," one of them confessed that July 3 afternoon. Yet "not a man flinched."

Virginia's Honored Sons

Pickett, Gettysburg, July 3, 1863 *(above)*

Pickett's division consisted of fifteen regiments almost entirely from the Piedmont and Tidewater regions of Virginia. The soldiers had more combat experience than did Pickett, although they had seen no action since Antietam nine months earlier. The three brigade commanders—Lewis A. Armistead, Richard B. Garnett, and James L. Kemper—were veteran soldiers of proven ability. In short, on July 3, Lee committed to battle one of the strongest elements in his army. Inside the ranks was the belief that "Pickett's Men" could and would, as Lee wrote in a letter to Gen. George T. Anderson, "carry anything they are put against."

All was ready when Pickett rode across the front of the line and told the soldiers: "Don't forget today that you are from Old Virginia!"

Col. William D. Stuart gave final instructions to his 56th Virginia: "Advance slowly with arms at will. No cheering. No firing. No breaking from common to quick step. Dress on the center. Forward, march!"

"Guides Center-March!"

Gen. Richard Garnett, Pickett's Charge, Gettysburg, July 3, 1863 *(below)*

For courtly and courteous Richard Garnett, the July 3 assault was his quest for vindication. A year earlier, he had been removed from command of the Stonewall Brigade on charges of disobedience that were never proven. Now he led Pickett's old brigade, and he did so with unusual eagerness.

Across the way, Federals four and five deep stood behind a rock wall. Charles Page of the 14th Connecticut was stunned as Pickett's division moved into the open. "It was a scene of unsurpassed grandeur and majesty," Page wrote. "... As far as the eye could reach could be seen the advancing troops, their gay war flags fluttering in the gentle summer breeze, while their sabers and bayonets flashed and glistened in the midday sun. Step by step they came.... Every movement expressed determination and resolute defiance, the line moving forward like a victorious giant, confident of power and victory."

There was an exception or two to those feelings. As the 18th Virginia started across that great field, Sam Paulett said to a comrade beside him: "This is going to be a heller! Prepare for the worst!"

"Steady, Boys, Steady!"

Gen. Lewis Armistead, Pickett's Charge, Gettysburg, July 3, 1863

Before the advance began, Garnett turned to Gen. Lewis Armistead and observed: "This is a desperate thing to attempt."

"It is," Armistead replied, "but the issue is with the Almighty, and we must leave it in His hands."

"Brave Old Lewis" Armistead was a longtime soldier who had come slowly up the ranks. (He had been expelled from West Point allegedly for hitting cadet Jubal Early with a dinner plate.) Armistead came to Gettysburg a forty-six-year-old widower who was both warmhearted and indomitable. He could be bluff and crusty because he was a no-nonsense soldier. He also looked after his men carefully, and they loved him for it.

On foot that afternoon, Armistead placed his hat on the tip of his sword. "Men!" he shouted. "Remember what you are fighting for! Remember your homes, your firesides, your wives, mothers, sisters and your sweethearts. Follow me!" He stepped forward twenty paces, waved the sword without looking back, and started out into the field.

The Fence

Pickett's Charge, Gettysburg, July 3, 1863

The area that was to be a battlefield bore the barrenness of death. North Carolina staff officer Louis Young complained: "The ground over which we had to pass was perfectly open, and numerous fences, some parallel and some oblique to our line of battle, were formidable impediments in our way."

To stop under fire and dismantle fences was out of the question. There was nothing to do but go over the top. Tennessean John H. Moore wrote: "The time it took to climb to the top of the fence seemed to me an age of suspense. It was not a leaping over; it was rather an insensible tumbling to the ground."

Worse, most of the fences were diagonal to the attack. Regiments went over them like a wave that breaks on a slanted beach. Unit formations began falling apart.

"On They Came with Flags Flying!"

Pickett's Charge, Gettysburg, July 3, 1863

Union Gen. Carl Schurz watched the unfolding drama through field glasses. "We could distinctly see the gaps torn in their ranks," he stated. "But the brave Rebels promptly filled the gaps . . . and unshaken and unhesitatingly, they continued their onward march." Musket fire blazed through dark gun smoke and gave an eerie lighting effect to the whole field. "Nearly every minute," a private in the 57th Virginia declared, "the cry of mortal agony was heard above the roar and rumble of guns."

The Confederates, now double-timing, appeared unstoppable. A major reason was Lewis Armistead. The men "caught his fire and determination," said the 9th Virginia's John H. Lewis. "It was his example, his coolness, his courage that led that brigade over that field of blood."

Bullets ripping through Armistead's hat—perched on his sword—caused it to slide down to the hilt, but the brigadier continued waving the blade.

He actually reached the Union line at the stone wall. However, brigade order had vanished. Fewer than a fourth of the Virginians were still pressing forward.

"The time it took to climb to the top of the fence

seemed to me an age of suspense."

—Lt. John H. Moore, 7th Tennessee

"Skilled troops on parade could not hold an alignment of line better....

There is no dismay, no discouragement, no wavering."

—Sgt. Patrick DeLacy, 143rd Pennsylvania

"To the Wall!" *(study, opposite, top)*

"Faster, Men, Faster!" *(opposite, bottom)*

Armistead, Pickett's Charge, Gettysburg, July 3, 1863

When Armistead lifted his sword to start the attack, he turned to color bearer Leander Blackburn. "Sergeant," he asked, "are you going to put those colors on the enemy's works today?" Blackburn answered: "I will try, sir, and if mortal man can do it, it shall be done!"

An "ocean of armed men" in gray and butternut under red battle flags and the blue banners of Virginia slowly moved forward. Marching at "common time" (ninety steps per minute) would take about twenty minutes to reach the Union positions. Armistead's regiments—in single column two rows deep—were eighty yards behind Garnett's brigade.

First, artillery tore through the ranks. Capt. Benjamin Farinholt of the 53rd Virginia watched a single shell leave a file of thirteen men "in a perfect mangled mass of flesh and blood indistinguishable one from the other."

Sgt. Blackburn fell dead early in the action. Four others who carried the same flag went down killed or wounded. Lt. Col. Rawley Martin reported: "The enemy behind the rock fence poured volley after volley into the advancing ranks. The men fell like stalks of grain before the reaper, but they closed the gaps and pressed forward, through the pitiless storm."

Fifty years later, Sgt. Patrick DeLacy of the 143rd Pennsylvania remembered: "Skilled troops on parade could not hold an alignment of line better. . . . There is no dismay, no discouragement, no wavering. It grows in magnificence as death's sting waxes stronger."

The Copse of Trees

Philadelphia Brigade at Pickett's Charge, Gettysburg, July 3, 1863

A little stand of scrub oak in the middle of the Union line on Cemetery Ridge became known as the Copse. It was the focal point of Pickett's Charge.

Manning that sector was Gen. Alexander Webb's Philadelphia Brigade. The three Pennsylvania regiments at hand numbered 940 men. They had been heavily engaged in the fighting of the previous day.

The brigade was not a model of discipline. (En route to the battle, its commander had issued stern orders against straggling, with a threat of the death penalty.) Nevertheless, the Pennsylvanians fought gallantly, suffering 47 percent casualties that day.

At the Copse, Webb's men waited until the attacking Confederates were barely fifty yards away before firing. "The slaughter was terrible," Cpl. John Buckley of the 69th Pennsylvania stated. Maj. Charles Peyton, whose 19th Virginia caught much of the musketry, wrote that his command "recoiled under the terrific fire that poured into our ranks."

"Try Them with the Bayonets!"

Pickett's Charge, Gettysburg, July 3, 1863 · "TRY THEM WITH THE BAYONETS!" *(study, below)*

The rising storm of Union fire soon turned neat columns into intermingled crowds. Southern ranks angled toward the copse of trees atop Cemetery Ridge. This move exposed them to a blistering artillery enfilade. "Many times a single percussion shell would cut out several files, and then explode in their ranks," Maj. Benjamin Rittenhouse of the 5th U.S. Artillery stated.

"Several times almost a company would disappear, as the shell would rip from the right to the left among them."

And the closer the Southerners came to the crest, the more intense became the Union musketry. The 1st Virginia's John Dooley, a veteran of two years' service, noted that gunfire was "breathing flame in our very faces" and the enemy's cannons were "thunder on our quivering melting ranks. Now truly does the work of death begin. The line becomes unsteady because at every step a gap must be closed."

"Follow Me, Boys!"

Armistead, Pickett's Charge, Gettysburg, July 3, 1863
"FOLLOW ME, BOYS!" *(study, right)*

As Armistead crouched at the wall, gunfire all around him, Col. Rawley Martin of the 53rd Virginia joined him. "Colonel, we can't stay here!" Armistead yelled. Martin agreed. Armistead turned to the one hundred men who had made it that far and cried out: "Come forward, Virginians! Come on, boys, we must give them the cold steel! Who will follow me?"

Over the wall they went. This unexpected breakthrough sent many of the Union soldiers scurrying to the rear. Armistead's band routed the 71st Pennsylvania and continued forward another 150 feet toward some abandoned field pieces. Armistead shouted for his men to turn the cannons on the Federals. Just as his hand touched one of the barrels, three bullets struck him.

Armistead died attacking the II Corps, commanded by his best friend in the prewar army, Winfield S. Hancock. What troops remained of the Virginians were shot, captured, or else retreated back across the wall. The breakthrough at the Copse lasted perhaps ten minutes.

The High Tide

Gettysburg, July 3, 1863 · THE HIGH TIDE *(study, below)*

It was Fredericksburg all over again, but this time in reverse.

The brigades of Garnett and James Kemper moved through a withering fire toward Cemetery Ridge. "They seemed impelled by some irresistible force," a foreign observer wrote. Union general Winfield Hancock stated that he had "never seen a more formidable attack," while Gen. Meade reported that "the assault was made with great firmness."

Three-fourths of the way across the field, Garnett's voice pierced through the roar: "Faster, men, faster! We are almost there!" Moments later, a fatal bullet through his forehead knocked Garnett from his horse.

Maj. Nathaniel Wilson shouted to his 28th Virginia: "Now, boys, put your trust in God and follow me!" He died seconds later.

Dennis O'Kane, colonel of the 69th Pennsylvania, had given the old Bunker Hill command to his men: "Don't shoot until you see the whites of their eyes!" His troops obeyed orders, with devastating effect.

A member of the 18th Virginia who lived to recall the assault wrote movingly: "Men fire into each other's faces not five feet apart. There are bayonet thrusts, saber strokes, pistol shots; cool, deliberate movements on the part of some—hot, passionate desperate efforts on the part of others; hand to hand contests; recklessness of life; tenacity of purpose; fiery determination; oaths, yells, curses, hurrahs, shoutings. . . . Seconds are centuries, minutes, ages."

The High Water Mark

Gettysburg, July 3, 1863

Of the Confederate attack, Virginia soldier George Finley stated sadly: "Men were falling all around us and cannon and muskets were raining death upon us. The 56th was being torn to pieces, but the men never faltered or wavered. They kept coming in strict formation. On and up the slope towards the stone wall the regiment . . . steadily swept, without a sound or a shot."

Heavily bearded Gen. James Kemper went down with a groin wound. All three of Pickett's brigades were without leadership, but soldiers continued fighting from instinct and for survival. One Union regiment, armed with carbines, fired so rapidly that the weapons became too hot to hold. Across a mile-square area, savage combat roared.

Ernest Linden Waitt, who compiled a history of the 19th Massachusetts in 1906, provides a horrifyingly vivid account of the melee: "Foot to foot, body to body and man to man they struggled, pushed, and strived and killed. Each had rather die than yield. The mass of wounded and heaps of dead entangled the feet of the contestants, and, underneath the trampling mass, wounded men who could no longer stand, struggled, fought, shouted and killed— hatless, coatless, drowned in sweat, black with powder, red with blood, stifling in the horrid heat, parched with smoke and blind with dust, with fiendish yells and strange oaths they blindly plied the work of slaughter."

"Foot to foot, **body to body** and man to man **they struggled, pushed, and strived and killed.**"

— Ernest Linden Waitt

The Angle

Gettysburg, July 3, 1863

It was the same at the Angle, where the stone wall made a right angle and formed a corner near the Copse. Johnston Pettigrew's division tried to make a breakthrough at that salient-like position.

There were no well-dressed ranks. The long advance across the field, the effort to negotiate Emmitsburg Road, and the deadly chore of crossing the fences left Southerners to push on singly or in small groups. The Emmittsburg Road ran obliquely through the battlefield, with traces of fences on either side. Worse, when Confederates reached the road, both sides knew that they were within range of Federal musket fire.

One of the units in place at the Angle was the 14th Connecticut.

As Pettigrew's men drew near, writer Charles D. Page recorded, "The word Fire! Fire! ran along the Union line, Crack! Crack! spoke out the musketry . . . and great gaps were formed in the [Confederate] line, the number of slain and wounded could not be estimated by numbers, but must be measured by yards. Yet on came the second line in full face of the awful carnage."

Lt. Col. John T. Jones of the 26th North Carolina acknowledged that "the storm of lead which now met us is beyond description." By the time the Carolinians got within fifty yards of the wall, wrote Thomas Cureton, the regiment "was reduced to a Skirmish line by the Constant falling of the Men at every Step."

The Repulse *(right)*
The Wreckage of War *(below)*

Gettysburg, July 3, 1863

Pickett's Charge ended because there were not enough men left to keep it going. The exhausted Confederate survivors—veteran soldiers who could stand some things but not everything—broke backward out of the smoke and drifted down the hill toward Seminary Ridge.

Charles Page wrote that the Federals were "now careless of shelter, stood erect and with loud shouts continued to fire into the retreating army as long as they were within range." The 56th Virginia's George Finley remarked: "The men who had begun to fall back seemed to be dropping as they ran, like leaves."

Losses had been appalling. Over 6,500 Southerners—more than half of all the men involved in the attack—had been killed, wounded, or captured in fighting that lasted barely an hour. Thirteen of Pickett's fifteen regimental commanders were lost.

The 18th Virginia numbered 341 soldiers at the outset of the charge; it lost 245 men, including 29 of its 31 officers. The 11th North Carolina, which had crossed the Potomac with 100 soldiers, was left with eight privates and a single officer.

"It's All My Fault"

Lee, Gettysburg, July 3, 1863 *(following pages)*

From three-quarters of a mile away, Lee watched the debris of the assault limping back across the field. He showed no expression as he rode to meet the survivors at the wood line. "Don't be discouraged," he kept saying; "it was all my fault this time. All good men must hold together."

It was late afternoon when a grief-stricken Pickett galloped up and announced half-hysterically that his division had been destroyed. "Come, General Pickett," Lee said quietly, "this has been my fault and upon my shoulders rests the blame. The men and officers of your command have written the name of Virginia today as high as it has ever been written before."

As Lee comforted his soldiers, no one stepped forward to comfort Lee. It was near 1 a.m. when his composure momentarily slipped. He stood in the darkness and exclaimed: "Too bad! Oh, too bad!"

Storm over Gettysburg

Lee and Longstreet, Gettysburg, July 3, 1863 *(top, left)*

Lee and Longstreet met once that night. Their conversation focused on extricating the army from Gettysburg.

After the failure of the third day's assault, Lee had no options left. His 28,000 casualties were too high, his ammunition and supplies too low, to remain longer in enemy territory. When Meade showed no inclination to attack on the morning of July 4, Lee said to an aide: "We must now return to Virginia."

Preparations were under way in early afternoon when a steady, pounding rain began anew. That added to the difficulty of getting ambulances and wagons heading southwest through the high country.

In his official report of the campaign, Lee stated proudly: "The privations and hardships of the march and camp were . . . borne with a fortitude unsurpassed by our ancestors in their struggle for independence, while their courage in battle entitles them to rank with the soldiers of any army and of any time."

Longstreet at Gettysburg

Longstreet and Staff *(top, right)*

The "slow and tenacious" James Longstreet was the anchor of the Army of Northern Virginia. Lee tended to give the orthodox work to his First Corps commander, a physically powerful and self-assertive man whose insensitiveness to public relations made him seem of an older generation. Fortunately, Longstreet surrounded himself with an excellent staff headed by Col. Moxley Sorrel of South Carolina.

While Sorrel praised Longstreet lavishly in his memoirs, he also wrote this summation of Longstreet's actions at Gettysburg: "Longstreet did not want to fight on the ground or on the plan adopted by the General-in-Chief. As Longstreet was not to be made willing and Lee refused to change or could not change, the former failed to conceal some anger. There was apparent apathy in his movements. They lacked the fire and point of his usual bearing on the battlefield."

Veterans of Gettysburg *(bottom)*

They had entered the army as innocent, impressionable young boys anxious to be good soldiers and eager for adventure. For large numbers of them, maturity came at Gettysburg. Recruits became veterans in a few bloody minutes.

With that maturity also came self-assurance. At Culp's Hill, Cemetery Ridge, and Little Round Top, Billy Yanks learned that while a great victory had been won, they had won it themselves. No one had ordered them to be courageous. The valor and the suffering came from something deep within their being.

Other battles remained yet to be fought, and many more soldiers would die along the way, but it was at Gettysburg that collections of brigades became an army at last—an army that would continue to exhibit the last full measure of devotion to cause and to country.

"The privations and **hardships** of the march and camp were . . .

borne with a fortitude unsurpassed by our

ancestors in their struggle for independence . . . "

—Gen. Robert E. Lee

The Long Road South

Fairfield, Pennsylvania, July 4, 1863

Rain fell unabated for two days. Roads became rivers of mud. Through that nightmare passed what Confederate general John Imboden termed a "vast procession of misery." Some 8,500 wounded soldiers were packed into wagons with neither springs nor bedding, and the procession bounced and jarred over rutted roads. The ambulance train was seventeen miles long. It took thirty-six hours for the train to pass a single point. Screams and moans were endless from one end to the other.

In just the first night's movement, Imboden wrote, "there was no time even to fill a canteen with water for a dying man; for, except for the drivers and the guards, all were wounded and utterly helpless in the vast procession of misery. During this one night I realized more of the horrors of war than I had in all the two preceding years."

Samuel Feamster of the 14th Virginia Cavalry was philosophical about the campaign. "I don't think we made much by going into Pennsylvania," he wrote home. "It was the darkest Hour we have ever had." Yet, he added hopefully, "the darkest hour is just before day."

" ... except for the drivers and the guards,

all were wounded and utterly

helpless in the vast procession of misery.

During this one night I realized more of

the horrors of war than I had in

all the two preceding years."

—Brig. Gen. John D. Imboden

CHAPTER FIVE

PATHS TO NORTHERN VICTORY

July 1863—April 1865

THE CONFEDERACY WAS BROKEN NOW. On July 4, 1863, as Gen. Robert E. Lee's battered army stumbled away from Gettysburg, Gen. Ulysses S. Grant completed a brilliant six-month campaign by capturing the river fortress of Vicksburg, Mississippi. The Southern nation was cut off from all of its land west of the Mississippi River. From St. Paul to the Gulf of Mexico, the great waterway was open to Union gunboats and transports.

More than loss of land shattered Confederate strength that summer. Gettysburg and Vicksburg cost the South some 50,000 men and 70,000 stands of arms—the equivalent of a full army. Such losses were irreplaceable by any measure. The South would continue to resist and would win some battles in the process, but the Confederacy lacked the resources to fulfill the insatiable appetite of war.

No fighting of consequence occurred in Virginia for the remainder of the year. Both armies had been crippled at Gettysburg, with neither able to do more than maneuver along the Virginian intrastate Orange and Alexandria Railroad.

With Virginia and Mississippi now the wings of the war front, eastern Tennessee became the center of attention. The focal point for both sides was Chattanooga, gateway to the lower Confederacy, a rail center located at the vital spot where the Tennessee River made a circular cut through the Cumberland Mountains.

Union forces under Maj. Gen. William S. Rosecrans moved on the city from different directions. Gen. Braxton Bragg and the Army of Tennessee retired southward twelve miles from the city. Rosecrans ignored Chattanooga to give chase. In doing so, he stumbled into a surprise attack by Confederates on September 19 along sluggish Chickamauga Creek. The two-day assault sent part of Rosecrans's army in wild retreat. A last-ditch stand by Maj. Gen. George H. Thomas's troops saved the Union army. Bragg's failure to follow up the success left the battle a hollow victory. The 34,000 total casualties represented a third of each army.

In November, two months later, with Rosecrans removed and Gen. Grant in command of a newly created Military Division of the Mississippi, Union soldiers moved on Chattanooga. Federals on November 24 scaled and seized Lookout Mountain, southwest of the city, breaking the left of the Confederate line. The next day, in heavy fighting, Grant drove Bragg in complete retreat from Missionary Ridge on the other flank. Chattanooga would become a major Union staging area for the remainder of the war.

The third year—1864—was the worst of all. Battle, once begun, remained uninterrupted. Death tolls increased to numbing heights. Destruction and desolation were commonplace. Defeat became something to be endured by the South.

Grant came east in March as the Union's new general-in-chief. He now commanded all of the Union armies, approximately 533,000 soldiers present for duty. The Army of the Potomac, not a Washington desk at the War Department, would be Grant's headquarters. His major problem initially was that he did not know the North's premier army, and it did not know him. Col. Charles Wainwright complained that in an early review Grant "rode along the line in a slouchy, unobservant way, with his coat unbuttoned and setting anything but an example of military bearing to the troops. There was no enthusiasm."

Appearance meant little to Grant—nor to the North, as events played out, for the unpretentious, slightly built general quickly devised the strategy that won the Civil War.

In the past, Grant stated, Union "armies in the East and West acted independently and without concert, like a balky team [of mules], no two ever pulling together." This lack of cooperation allowed Confederates to shift from one point to another to meet the most pressing danger, and "to furlough large numbers, during seasons of inactivity on our part, to go to their homes and do the work of producing, for the support of their armies." Such would no longer be the case. Union command would strike wherever it could with all the force it had, and all of the blows would be coordinated. This strategy was elementary, but it had never been done before.

At the beginning of May, the Union navies began tightening their holds on the rivers and at sea. William T. Sherman, Grant's favorite general and now in command of the West, started south with three armies. His objective was Atlanta, the second most important supply base left in the Confederacy.

A multipronged Union offensive began simultaneously in Virginia. A mounted Federal force in West Virginia started through the mountains to cut the Virginia and Tennessee Railroad, Richmond's only link with the West. Maj. Gen. Franz Sigel, a German emigrant and former Baden military leader, moved into the Shenandoah Valley. A new Army of the James started up Virginia's James River with Richmond as its target. Grant and the Army of the Potomac crossed the Rapidan River to take on Lee.

At first, nothing succeeded for Grant. The railroad in southwest Virginia was only momentarily severed; Sigel's advance up the valley came to an inglorious defeat at New Market; Maj. Gen. Benjamin Butler's move along the James vacillated between ineffectiveness and failure. In the first week of May, the main Union army was easing through the tangled woodland known as the Wilderness when Lee suddenly attacked on two parallel roads.

Forty-eight hours of intense fighting, climaxed by the timely arrival of James Longstreet's corps from Tennessee, produced another stunning defeat for the Army of the Potomac.

Yet this time there was no retreat. The war had changed; so had Union leadership. Grant was going to keep after Lee's army—to fight it whenever possible until one side could fight no more.

From the Wilderness, Grant launched one sledgehammer attack after another: Spotsylvania, North Anna, Cold Harbor. Unable to take Richmond by frontal assault, Grant crossed the James River in an attempt to seize Petersburg, twenty-three miles south of the capital, to get at its soft underbelly. Yet Lee arrived with his army just in time to block this advance.

A month's fighting in Virginia had produced 50,000 Union casualties, roughly two of every four soldiers in Meade's Army of the Potomac. On the other hand, Federals had inflicted 32,000 losses in Lee's army (almost half of his strength). Lee had fought superbly, but he was losing the war. Grant had seized the initiative, forced Lee halfway across the state, taken away Southern mobility, and strapped Lee's manpower and supplies.

Grant then turned to the siege warfare that had served him well at Vicksburg. For the next nine and a half months, the two armies stared across a deadly no-man's land on the Richmond-Petersburg front. Time was all on the Union side.

Sherman also fared poorly at the outset of spring 1864. It took two months for his forces to move one hundred miles to the outskirts of Atlanta. Then, two heavy, ill-conceived Confederate attacks on July 20 and 22 were routed by the Federals. Sherman began a slow envelopment of the city. On September 2, Confederates abandoned Atlanta. Union seizure of the city went far in ensuring President Lincoln's reelection in the autumn.

To demonstrate that the Confederacy was too weak to live, Sherman burned Atlanta and set out with 60,000 soldiers on a 285-mile "march to the sea." His forty-mile-wide advance cut a path of destruction to Savannah. Confederate efforts to pull Sherman back by making an offensive in Tennessee were unsuccessful. George H. Thomas's army inflicted near-fatal blows to the Confederate army, first at Franklin and then at Nashville. Early in 1865, an unmolested Sherman then proceeded northward through the Carolinas.

The end came quickly in Virginia. On April 2, Grant unleashed his forces in an all-out attack in Petersburg that fractured Lee's thin lines. A general retreat westward began, with Lee's hungry and careworn troops limping in search of refuge and Grant's army snapping at flanks and rear. By April 9, Lee had nowhere to go. Grant's lenient surrender terms eased the start of the healing process.

Sherman accepted the surrender of the Army of Tennessee later in the month. As spring melted into summer, the echo of gunfire died away. The South in general and Virginia in particular lay ravaged. A new Union got on its feet and began to take unsteady steps forward.

"Fondly do we hope

—fervently do we pray—

that this mighty scourge of war may

speedily pass away."

—Pres. Abraham Lincoln,
Second Inaugural Address,
March 4, 1865

The Glorious Fourth

Gen. Ulysses S. Grant, Vicksburg, Mississippi, July 4, 1863

At 10:30 a.m., July 4, 1863, U. S. Grant sent the War Department a succinct telegram that began: "The Enemy surrendered this morning."

Behind the statement was a six-week siege that had reduced Vicksburg to a squalid, starving hellhole. Included in the capture were 29,500 Confederate soldiers, 172 cannons, and 60,000 rifles and muskets.

Grant made a brief ride into Vicksburg just before noon. He was on his favorite mount, Cincinnati, and chewing one of his fourteen daily cigars. The Midwestern soldiers of his army cheered so lustily that Grant embarrassedly lifted his hat in acknowledgement.

"The fate of the Confederacy was sealed when Vicksburg fell," Grant wrote in his memoirs. Lincoln saw additional joy in the victory. At last he had found a general who could win, and win decisively. On July 5, the president declared: "Grant is my man, and I am his for the rest of the war."

"We intend to **live off the Yankees,** hereafter, and let them feel ... some of the **horrors** of war."

—Sgt. Henry Stone

Morgan's Ohio Raid

Montgomery, Ohio, July 14, 1863

A Nashville maiden once announced that she would rather have a kiss from John Hunt Morgan than a wedding proposal from the wealthiest officer in the Union army. By 1863 the famed Kentucky Cavalier was well on his course of raiding for its own sake. Anti-Union encouragement from the Midwestern states led Morgan to take his greatest gamble of the war: a 1,100-mile foray across southern Indiana and Ohio.

Against orders, on July 8 Morgan led 2,460 horsemen on a three-week expedition daring in conception and incredible in its folly. "We intend to live off the Yankees, hereafter," Sgt. Henry Stone asserted, "and let them feel . . . some of the horrors of war." The Confederates behaved as badly as Yankee guerrillas. They confiscated horses, stole food and forage, and looted indiscriminately. At Montgomery, Ohio (pictured), Morgan's men rode off with hats, a birdcage, and bolts of cloth.

Increasing numbers of Federal cavalry finally brought Morgan to bay. He and most of his command were captured and dumped unceremoniously in the Ohio state penitentiary. Morgan escaped shortly thereafter and resumed his partisan ranger tactics until his death the following year

The Autograph Seekers of Bel Air

Gen. Lee, Front Royal, Virginia, July 22, 1863 *(following pages)*

Lee was recovering from the losses at Gettysburg when, on July 22, he stopped at Bel Air, the Buck family mansion on the outskirts of Front Royal, Virginia. He relaxed briefly on the front porch with family members, including daughters Lucy and Ellen (known as Nellie).

"Before leaving," Lucy wrote in her diary, "he enriched Nellie's autograph book and mine with his name protesting that he knew we would much prefer having our sweethearts' there rather than his. Dear old General! I've always admired and loved him, but what a filial reverence mingles with that feeling now and how much more the father than the general he seems. How his hair is silvered and his brow marked with thought and care, yet what a noble, benevolent spirit looks forth from his brown eyes. What an air of dignity about his every movement."

Eye of the Storm

Gen. Patrick Cleburne, Battle of Chickamauga, Tennessee and Georgia, September 19, 1863

A few miles southeast of Chattanooga, Chickamauga Creek meandered through thick woodland. There, for two days in September, the armies of William Rosecrans and Braxton Bragg waged a vicious battle along a three-mile front.

Gen. Patrick Cleburne, a tough Irish veteran of the British army, led an oversize Confederate division that was one of the crack units of the Civil War. After nightfall on the first day's action, Cleburne's men forded the icy creek in water that was armpit deep, then attacked the Union's left flank. L. N. Williams of the 33rd Alabama noted that "there was one solid, unbroken wave of awe-inspiring sound. It seemed as if the fires of earth and hell had been turned loose in one mighty effort to destroy each other."

Hand-to-hand fighting occurred in the dark woods. Each side aimed at the flashes of the other guns. Cleburne seized a mile of ground, three cannon, and some 300 prisoners before "confusion at the time, necessarily inseparable . . . from a night attack" ended the contest.

His division, wet and weary, spent the cold night on the battleground.

The Gettysburg Address

Pres. Abraham Lincoln, Gettysburg, Pennsylvania, November 19, 1863 *(opposite)*

November 19, 1863, was a warm and pleasant Thursday. More than 12,000 people crowded into Gettysburg, Pennsylvania. The governors of eighteen Northern states had appointed trustees to establish a new cemetery where the hastily buried dead of July's battle might be reinterred. Famed orator Edward Everett—who among many achievements served as a Massachusetts representative, senator, and governor, U.S. secretary of state, and president of Harvard—was to deliver a suitable speech. The president of the United States would dedicate the ground as a national shrine.

Everett spoke two hours; Lincoln, barely two minutes. (A photographer was still fussing with his tripod when the president finished his remarks and sat down.) Yet what Lincoln called his "little speech" became the greatest address in American history.

In 268 well-chosen words, Lincoln spoke of liberty and equality rather than of victory. We must never forget those who "gave the last full measure of devotion," he emphasized. The beliefs that gave birth to the nation were the strengths that, rededicated and held true, would guide its future. By that path, Lincoln concluded, "that government of the people, by the people, for the people, shall not perish from the earth."

Lincoln made one deviation from the prepared remarks. He inserted the phrase "under God" in the statement: "that this nation shall have a new birth of freedom."

By sunset, a reverent stillness had settled over Gettysburg.

"Your fathers marched through suffering, privation, and blood,

to Independence! ... Be assured that the just God, who crowned their efforts with

success, will in His own good time, send down His blessings upon yours."

—From a circular distributed by Gen. Lee to his troops

Sunrise Service

Religion was the greatest sustainer of morale in the Civil War. Men either carried faith with them into service, or they discovered the need for God amid the terrors of battle and sickness.

Fully a fourth of Lee's army took an active role in a religious revival that surged through the ranks that winter. Faith in God's will likewise helped civilians weather the pangs of uncertainty and despair. Inside a church, wives, sweethearts, and mothers could feel a spiritual closeness to loved ones far away. The lyrics of old hymns suddenly took on new meaning: "O God, our help in ages past / Our hope for years to come / Our shelter from the stormy blast / And our eternal home."

Southern Stars

Kernstown, Virginia, Winter 1862 *(above)*

At the Opequon Presbyterian Church in Kernstown, Virginia, an evening service had just concluded when a column of horsemen rode past on patrol. It was a touching scene of peace and war.

Soldier of Faith

Lee, Orange Court House, Virginia, February 17, 1864 *(right)*

The winter of 1863–64 was a somber one for Lee. Trying to patch an army battered at Gettysburg and filling dozens of officer slots made vacant by death, wounds, and sickness were only part of the problem. "A brigade that recently went on picket," Lee informed the quartermaster general, was "compelled to leave several hundred men in camp who were unable to bear the exposure of duty, being destitute of shoes and blankets."

Lee's headquarters that winter was a cluster of tents "on a wooded hill just east" of the town of Orange Court House. The Rapidan River was the Confederate line of defense. Lee often attended worship services at St. Thomas Episcopal Church in the village.

On a snowy night in February, Lee rode quietly by the church. With Lee, Chaplain J. William Jones wrote, "vital godliness was a precious reality." Only three weeks earlier, Lee had sought to reassure his troops with a circular that stated in part: "Your fathers marched through suffering, privation, and blood, to Independence! . . . Be assured that the just God, who crowned their efforts with success, will in His own good time, send down His blessings upon yours."

Battle Above the Clouds

Lookout Mountain, Tennessee, November 24, 1863

Lookout Mountain—towering a thousand feet over Chattanooga, a horseshoe bend in the Tennessee River, and a major railroad—seemed too formidable for conquest. In addition, wrote one Confederate, the mountain was "all gorges, boulders, and jutting cliffs."

That is why Bragg's defenses along the slopes were so thin. That is why Union forces attacked it in the morning fog of November 24. "We were enjoying the fun of our fancied security," Robert Jamison of the 45th Tennessee recalled, "when suddenly we heard the rattle of small arms."

Federals in numbers approximately six times those of the defenders swarmed up the rocks, around crevices, and through fog mixed with gun smoke. Confederate cannons could not be effectively depressed to fire downhill—the balls rolled out of the barrels before detonation—while Union guns delivered a punishing barrage. Federal division commander John Geary wrote: "Our fire was delivered in continuous volleys, and, with walls of steel, colors and men were over the works and hand to hand [combat dispatched] the enemy's possession of them."

Near noon the gun smoke drifted away, the fog lifted, and the Stars and Stripes could clearly be seen flying on the mountain crest. Newspapers exaggerated the fight by calling it the "battle above the clouds." Nevertheless, it broke the last Confederate hold on Chattanooga.

The Final Mission

CSS *H. L. Hunley,* Charleston, South Carolina, February 17, 1864

From the beginning, the Confederacy lacked the resources to keep pace with Northern shipbuilding. It experimented with a number of revolutionary innovations. One was the first underwater vessel to sink an enemy warship.

The CSS *H. L. Hunley* was approximately forty feet long and four feet in diameter. Steam power was not possible. Seven men hand-cranked the propeller while the captain controlled depth and steered the vessel by sightings through a glass port in the hatch cover. A spar torpedo was its sole weapon.

In the experimental stage at Charleston, the *Hunley* sank on two different occasions, killing thirteen men. Nevertheless, on February 17, 1864, with calm seas and a favorable tide, the *Hunley* eased from her berth and made her way across Charleston harbor toward the ring of Union blockade ships. Around 8 p.m. she rammed the USS *Housatonic,* a new wooden steam sloop. The Federal vessel sank in five minutes. The *Hunley* also disappeared, not to be located until 1995. The remains of the crew were still inside.

James R. McClintock, the boat's principal designer, never lost his vision of such a revolutionary craft. "Since the war," he noted, "I have thought over the subject considerable and am satisfied that the Power can easily be obtained . . . to make the submarine Boat the most formidable enemy of Marine warfare ever known."

Thirteenth Amendment Is Passed

April 8, 1864

The Emancipation Proclamation unlocked the door to abolition, but getting through it for good proved a difficult task. Would a wartime decree by the president hold up against postwar challenges?

In April 1864, at Lincoln's prodding, the Senate cleared a thirteenth amendment abolishing slavery by a 38–6 vote. In the House of Representatives, however, Northern so-called Copperhead Democrats and border-state conservatives opposed passage as an encroachment on state rights. The vote there was 93–65, thirteen votes short of the necessary two-thirds. Any adoption by the House would have to come at the next session of Congress.

On January 11, 1865, after intense lobbying and a reminder by a Democratic congressman that his colleagues had suffered political defeats in the autumn elections "because we [would] not venture to cut loose from the dead carcass of negro slavery," the measure passed on a 119–56 vote. In the packed

galleries, this first amendment to the Constitution in sixty years evoked loud cheers. Blacks embraced and wept with joy.

Ratification by the states became official in December 1865. It was the first amendment to make a radical change in American society. One could also say that it was the final shot of the Civil War.

"Neither slavery nor involuntary servitude,

except as a punishment for crime whereof the party shall have been duly convicted,

shall exist within the United States,

or any place subject to their jurisdiction."

—Section 1 of the Thirteenth Amendment

Background: Detail of the original Thirteenth Amendment document signed by Pres. Lincoln and Congress, courtesy the Library of Congress, Abraham Lincoln Papers.

Sheridan's Men

The successful general molds his men into his own image.

Philip Sheridan, son of Irish immigrants, was always a fighter. An altercation with a fellow cadet at West Point cost him an extra year at the academy. He served on frontier duty until the outbreak of civil war. A no-nonsense, humorless, aggressive leader, Sheridan demanded the same qualities in his soldiers.

In 1864 Grant brought Sheridan to Virginia to overhaul Union cavalry. The tough little man did so. Swinging his horsemen like some giant scythe, he made a dashing raid on Richmond and killed Confederate Gen. Jeb Stuart in one of the actions. Weeks later,

Sheridan's men turned the lower end of the Shenandoah Valley into "a barren waste."

Sheridan's cold determination and profane ways were widely known—and sometimes appreciated. Col. Joshua Lawrence Chamberlain recalled that in the last weeks of the war, "we had a taste of General Sheridan's fighting style, and we liked it. . . . He transfuses into his subordinates the vitality and energy of his purpose, transforms them into part of his own mind and will. He shows the power of a commander."

Many soldiers asserted that there never was a fight quite like the Wilderness. "It was a battle which no man could see, and whose progress could only be followed by the ear," one Union private said. Charging men did not know where the enemy was until they ran right into them. The roar of musketry came from every direction. Woods were too dense, smoke too heavy, to make sense of the scene. Worse, the dry woods caught fire. Waves of flames rolled across the ground, cremating soldiers too injured to move to safety. Grant's losses were greater than Union casualties at Fredericksburg and equal to those in six days of fighting at Chancellorsville.

On the night of May 7, with the Wilderness still burning, Grant and Meade mounted their horses and proceeded to a crossroads, where they turned south. That ninety-degree turn was one of the critical decisions of the war.

There would be no retreat this time, no withdrawal to come back and perhaps fight later. Grant would continue advancing, looking for Lee, and fighting when they met. Union soldiers recognized this determination, and they hollered loudly—not the parade-ground cheers of young recruits but veterans' yells of respect. The plain-looking, emotionless Grant ordered them to be quiet, lest the Rebels detect a movement under way.

Lincoln, when later asked what sort of man Grant was, replied: "He's the quietest little fellow you ever saw. . . . The only evidence you have that he's in any place is that he makes things git! Wherever he is, things move!"

Tender Is the Heart

Gens. Lee and Hill, Orange Court House, Virginia, May 1, 1864

In the dark chasms of war, a tender moment sometimes intrudes. A baptism took place on Sunday, May 1, 1864. It was a private, extraordinary ceremony.

Robert E. Lee rode to the Orange County headquarters of corps commander Powell Hill, whom Lee regarded as "the best soldier of his grade with me." Hill's wife Kitty, a sister of Gen. John Hunt Morgan, had given birth six months earlier to their third daughter. In honor of Hill's sister and the man he most admired, Hill named the baby Lucy Lee.

Rev. Richard Davis of St. Thomas Episcopal Church in Orange Court House performed the baptismal rite. Lee was godfather and tenderly held the child in his arms throughout most of the service.

Lucy Lee married but was childless. At her death in 1931, the Hill line died with her. She took pride in her father's reputation for aggressiveness, and she was quick to be resentful if someone suggested that his aggressiveness was impetuosity. Just before she died, Lucy pleaded: "I do so want to have justice done my father. It never has been."

"He's the quietest little

fellow you ever saw. . . . The only evidence

you have that he's in any place is that

he makes things git!

Wherever he is, things move!"

—Pres. Abraham Lincoln, on Gen. Ulysses S. Grant

The Bloody Angle

Spotsylvania, Virginia, May 12, 1864

Both armies moved speedily ten miles from the Wilderness to Spotsylvania, a country town, like Gettysburg, where a number of roads met. Lee arrived first and quickly built fortifications. Skirmishing all too soon became an enormous fight that lasted ten uninterrupted days.

On May 12 occurred possibly the most vicious battle of the entire war. Hand-to-hand combat raged for eighteen hours, in pelting rain and deepening mud, for a horseshoe-shaped arc in the Southern lines. Men fought with bayonets and clubbed muskets for control of a few hundred yards of earthworks. Dead and wounded soldiers sank out of sight in the mud. Blood and rain were intermixed. "Never before on earth," historian Bruce Catton stated, "had so many muskets been fired so fast for so narrow a front and at such close range. About all that kept the two armies from completely annihilating each other was the fact that most men were firing too rapidly to aim."

When the long day ended, over 7,000 Federals and an equal number of Confederates had been lost. Grant had momentarily gained the "bloody angle," a square mile of useless ground.

Georgia veteran William Bass told his wife: "You can imagine what a hard struggle it [was] when I say Gettysburg cannot be compared to it." A Maine officer, Thomas Hyde, could not capture the frightening spectacle. "I never expect to be fully believed when I tell what I saw of the horrors of Spotsylvania, because I should be loath to believe it myself were the case reversed."

"I never expect to be fully believed when

I tell what I saw of the horrors

of Spotsylvania, because

I should be loath to believe it myself

were the case reversed."

—Lt. Col. Thomas W. Hyde, 7th Maine

"I think he was **the handsomest man** I ever saw."

—Capt. Job Parsons, 18th Virginia, on Maj. Gen. John C. Breckenridge

Thunder in the Valley

Battle of New Market, Virginia, May 15, 1864 *(opposite)*

Gen. Franz Sigel failed in a task he should have never been given. As part of Grant's overall 1864 strategy, Sigel led a sizable Union force southward up the Shenandoah Valley. The Confederate commander of the district was Kentuckian John C. Breckenridge, former vice president of the United States.

Maj. Gen. Breckenridge gathered in every military unit he could find, including 261 cadets from the Virginia Military Institute. On May 15, amid a steady rainstorm, and outnumbered three to two in manpower, Breckenridge boldly attacked. Capt. Job Parsons of the 18th Virginia Cavalry looked at the general in his rubberized raincoat and stated: "I think he was the handsomest man I ever saw."

Sigel's defenses were unprepared. The Union line began to give, then broke apart. The VMI cadets were part of the triumphant final assault. Ten of the teenagers were killed and forty-seven wounded. Sigel became so discombobulated by the action that he began shouting orders in German.

Seldom did so small a victory make such a large impact. Had Sigel been left unchallenged, he might easily have conquered the valley and brought starvation to Lee's army.

Charge at Trevilian Station

Gen. Wade Hampton and the Cadet Rangers, Louisa County, Virginia, June 11, 1864

With Union general Philip Sheridan's cavalry roaming through the Virginia Piedmont, Lee responded by sending two-thirds of his mounted force under Wade Hampton to intercept the threat. Hampton was the very picture of a patrician warrior: a militarily untrained South Carolina plantation magnate who had a native military ability that steadily improved with experience. Longstreet's chief of staff thought Hampton "of fine presence, a bold horseman, a swordsman, and of the most undaunted courage."

Hampton caught Sheridan at Trevilian Station, a stop on the Virginia Central Railroad, on June 11, and for two days the fighting was close-quartered and bloody. A climax to the first day's action came when Hampton personally led a dramatic charge with the 6th South Carolina Cavalry. One of its companies was the Cadet Rangers, students from The Citadel, South Carolina's military academy.

Sheridan abandoned the campaign and started on a wide sweep back to Grant's army. Trevilian Station was an encouraging success when the South needed it, and the battle stamped Hampton as a worthy successor to the fallen Jeb Stuart.

Shenandoah Sunrise

Battle of Cedar Creek, Virginia, October 19, 1864

Gen. Philip Sheridan became the third commander Grant sent to clear the Shenandoah Valley. He inflicted two defeats on the Confederate army, then leisurely encamped at Cedar Creek some twenty miles south of Winchester.

At dawn on October 19, Gen. Jubal Early launched a surprise attack that sent the Union army racing down the road in disorganized retreat. Gen. John B. Gordon, an untrained soldier who was Georgia's greatest general, galloped up to Belle Grove, Sheridan's headquarters, and sought to keep the attack going. Yet human need had overcome military necessity. Hundreds of

Confederates were barefoot, everyone was ragged, and none had eaten a square meal in weeks. The fully stocked, abandoned Union camp was "the great temptation" that reduced half of Early's army into "a plundering mob."

At that juncture, Sheridan rushed onto the field and led a heavy counterattack. The Southern army, wrote Gordon, broke apart "like hard clods of clay under a pelting rain." The 21st Virginia's Samuel Sublett later wrote his sister: "On that day our Army won the greatest victory of this war, & the same day was more disgracefully beaten than an Army ever was."

Sheridan's Ride

Battle of Cedar Creek, Virginia, October 19, 1864

His most dramatic hour came at Cedar Creek, when he personally turned a routed force into a victorious army.

Philip Sheridan looked the part of an unfeeling fighter. Only five feet, four inches tall, he was a tough little man with black hair, olive-dark face, heavy mustache, and hard eyes. Abraham Lincoln (himself a physical wonder) once described Sheridan as "a brown, chunky, little chap, with a long body, short legs, not enough neck to hang him, and such long arms that if his ankles itch he can scratch them without stooping."

Sometimes Sheridan stormed and raged; at other times he fidgeted and glared. Yet he always approached combat with cold dedication.

Battle for the Shenandoah

May–October 1864

In unoccupied areas of the military theaters, cavalry competed with infantry for supremacy. Mounted soldiers had traditionally been used for reconnaissance and screening an army. That changed as the Civil War became more encompassing.

For the first half of the struggle, Confederate horsemen were so superior to Union troopers that no real comparison existed. Union Gen. William T. Sherman once exclaimed: "Give me Southern cavalry and Union infantry, and I will conquer the world."

Southerners were from rural areas and accustomed to horses. Legends of chivalry were so powerful in the South that it seemed more knightly to enter the war as a cavalryman on your own

mount. Union cavalry, in contrast, mostly obtained recruits from nonagricultural regions who first had to be taught how to stay in the saddle.

By 1863 the North's numerical superiority in men and mounts, plus experience and better training, shifted the balance. Major cavalry actions at Brandy Station and Gettysburg heralded the age of Union cavalry. The following year, notably in the Virginia Piedmont and the Shenandoah Valley, hundreds of mounted soldiers clashed with sabers and pistols in running battles of dramatic scope.

And, of course, the horses got the worst of it in every fight.

"War Is Hell"

Gen. William T. Sherman, Atlanta, Georgia, November 15, 1864

More than Grant or Sheridan, William T. Sherman believed in total war. To conquer, one must destroy everything—civilian as well as military—that could contribute to the power to resist. In a postwar speech to Union veterans, Sherman asserted: "There is many a boy here today who looks on war as all glory, but, boys, it is all hell."

Sherman fully demonstrated that belief after occupying Atlanta. The next objective, he felt, was to defeat the Southern spirit that sustained the Confederacy. If he could drive destructively through the Georgia heartland all the way to the Atlantic coast, that would be conclusive proof of a Southern nation no longer capable of defending itself. Citizens will "raise a howl against my barbarity and cruelty," Sherman told the

War Department, but "I will answer that war is war and not popularity-seeking."

On November 15, Sherman left Atlanta after ordering everything of military value burned. Inevitably, the flames spread and enveloped the whole city. William Calkins of the 104th Illinois remembered fires "illuminating the whole heavens . . . the pandemonium caused by the flames, the yells of the soldiery, the explosion of shells and ammunition."

Sherman was standing on a hill overlooking the burning city as his troops filed past. A band struck up "John Brown's Body," and the soldiers began to sing. "Never before or since," Sherman later wrote, "have I heard the chorus of 'Glory, glory, hallelujah!' done with more spirit, or in better harmony of time and place."

Confederate Crossing

Gen. Nathan Bedford Forrest,
Owen's Ford, Tennessee,
November 28, 1864

Viscount Garnet Wolseley—
a visitor to the South who in
1895 became commander in
chief of Her Majesty's forces—
concluded a study of Gen. Bedford Forrest with the observation:
"He trained his men to make war after his own fashion, but he
drilled them very little, because he knew nothing of drill itself. He
applied his own common sense to carry out the war instinct that
was in him. His mind was not narrowed by military apothegms.
. . . He knew what he wanted to accomplish, and he went for that
object with all the cunning of an Indian and all the common sense
of a business man."

When Sherman abandoned Atlanta, the Confederate army
moved into Tennessee in a desperate effort to lure Sherman out of
Georgia. Gen. John B. Hood reached Columbia, forty miles south
of Nashville. He sent Forrest's cavalry on a long swing around the
Union left.

The effort failed, but not from want of trying. Union Col.
Henry Stone stated that the weather was "of great severity. It
rained and snowed and hailed and froze, and the roads were
almost impassable. Forrest had come up . . . and led the advance
with indomitable energy."

Bringing Cleburne In

Franklin, Tennessee, December 1, 1864 *(below)*

It was an attack as spectacular and as hopeless as Pickett's assault
at Gettysburg. On the Indian-summer afternoon of November 30,
Hood sent 28,000 Confederates forward in a head-on charge at the
heavily entrenched Federals. The outcome was never in doubt.
Twelve generals and fifty-four regimental colonels were among the
6,300 Southern men slain, wounded, or captured.

Among the six Southern generals killed was the "Stonewall
of the West," Patrick Cleburne. His bravery was legendary to the
end. He led his division into the attack. When his horse fell dead,
Cleburne began mounting another when that horse was killed. He
was last seen "moving forward on foot, waving his cap." His body
was recovered the next morning.

Cleburne had tried earnestly to talk Hood out of making the
attack. When that failed, he moved to the front of the battle line
and said: "If we are to die, let us die like men."

"If we are to die, let us die like men."

—Gen. Patrick Cleburne

While the Enemy Rests

Col. John Mosby's Rangers, Paris Mountain, Virginia, December 1, 1864

Innocent civilians and law-abiding farmers for days at a time, when Col. John Mosby's battalion of rangers gathered for action they became hell-raising guerrillas who feasted on Union supply trains, picket posts, culverts, bridges, and couriers. The rangers came largely from the northern Virginia counties of Fauquier and Loudoun. Although behind enemy lines most of the war, the area was known as Mosby's Confederacy after the man who controlled it.

Slight, wiry, cold-eyed, Mosby fought with absolute fearlessness. Some 1,900 men served in his command, but Mosby usually operated with no more than 800 horsemen at a time. Thousands of Federal troops were diverted to guard against the little colonel, and Grant angrily directed that any Mosby man captured could be executed without trial. Nothing deterred Mosby's activities.

One Union officer declared: "A more harassing enemy could not well be imagined." Another stated of the rangers: "They were a most dangerous element, and caused perhaps more loss than any single body of men in the enemy's service."

The Gunner and
the Colonel

Battle of Fort Fisher, North Carolina,
January 15, 1865

Fort Fisher, a sprawling, sand-dune fortification,
defended the Cape Fear River and Wilmington, North
Carolina, the one open seaport left to the Confederacy.
Union attempts to take Fort Fisher in December 1864
failed. A month later, following two days of naval
bombardment led by Adm. David Porter—which was
termed "beyond description,"—6,000 to 9,000 Union
soldiers assaulted Fort Fisher and its 1,500 defenders.

Battle began in mid-afternoon on January 13.
"The fight was no doubt the closest and longest of the
war," New York soldier Hermon Clarke wrote his
father. "It was hand-to-hand for nearly six hours."

Col. Newton Curtis (one of the tallest Civil War
soldiers at six feet, six inches) led the major attack with
a saber in one hand and the 117th New York flag in the
other. A sole Confederate gunner stood defiantly beside
a huge ten-inch Columbiad gun until he was struck
down. Curtis lost his left eye from a shell fragment.

A Union surgeon observed: "If the roar of artillery
abated, it was more than supplied by the yelling and
the din of deadly musketry. All along the crest of the
parapet . . . might be seen the desperate contest."

Weight of numbers proved decisive. Fort Fisher's
commander surrendered at 10 p.m. on the fifteenth,
thereby closing the South's last door to the outer world.

"**The fight** was no doubt the

closest and longest of the war. It

was hand-to-hand for

nearly six hours."

—Lt. Hermon Clarke,
117th New York

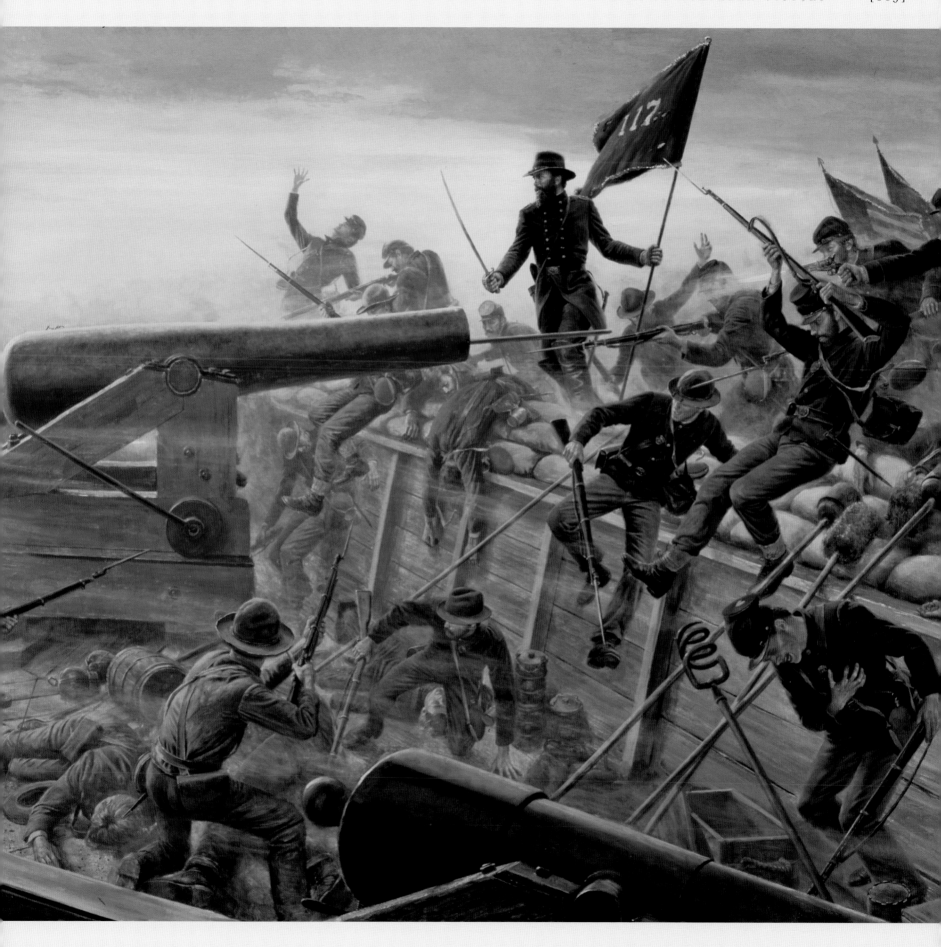

Malice Toward None

Lincoln's Second Inaugural, March 4, 1865

March 4, 1865, Inauguration Day at the White House, began wet and windy, but the sun dramatically broke through the clouds just before Lincoln gave the shortest and most memorable inaugural address in American history.

He could easily have used the occasion to lash out at his critics from North and South. On the eve of victory, expressions of arrogance or vindictiveness might have been appropriate. Instead, the address was remarkably impersonal. The future lay with God, Lincoln declared. "Fondly do we hope—fervently do we pray—that this mighty scourge of war may speedily pass away." With unmatched eloquence the president concluded: "With malice toward none; with charity for all; with firmness in the right, as God gives us to see the right, let us strive on to finish the work we are in; to bind up the nation's wounds; . . . to do all which may achieve and cherish a just, and a lasting peace, among ourselves, and with all nations."

Thunderous applause broke the stillness. The *Washington National Intelligencer* asserted that Lincoln's words, "equally distinguished for patriotism, statesmanship, and benevolence," deserved "to be printed in gold."

Lincoln's Inaugural Ball

White House, Washington, D.C., March 5, 1865 *(opposite)*

At the mobbed reception and ball at the White House held on March 5, 1865, the day after the inauguration, Lincoln reportedly shook hands with four thousand well-wishers. Mary Lincoln's

presence was conspicuous. She used the occasion to emerge from three years' mourning for Willie, who had died of typhoid fever at the age of eleven—the second Lincoln son to die tragically young.

Untold numbers shoved their way all through the presidential mansion. "The White House," wrote bodyguard William Crook, "looked as if a regiment of rebel troops had been quartered there—with permission to forage."

The physically exhausted Lincoln held up well throughout the grueling ordeal, beaming when noted black orator Frederick Douglass called his inaugural address "a sacred effort." Other guests felt concern: the president looked not only old, but feeble. Mrs. Lincoln also worried. "Poor Mr. Lincoln is looking so broken-hearted, so completely worn out," she told her dressmaker. "I fear he will not get through the next four years."

"With malice toward none; with charity for all;...

let us ... do all which may achieve and cherish a just, and a lasting peace,

among ourselves, and with all nations."

—Pres. Abraham Lincoln, from Second Inaugural Address

The Last Rally

Lee, Sayler's Creek, Virginia, April 6, 1865

In the first days of April, Lee's broken army slogged westward from Petersburg with ever-decreasing speed. Hunger, weariness, and depression engulfed the ranks. Debris and stragglers lay in the wake as the pursuing Union army constantly jabbed and sliced at the column.

Federals spied a gap in Lee's line at Sayler's Creek on April 6 and quickly moved through it. A full third of the Confederate army was isolated. Almost 8,000 men were captured because of the absolute hopelessness of their situation.

Lee rode upon the scene in time to see running toward him teamsters without wagons, soldiers without guns, officers without commands. "My God!" Lee exclaimed. "Has the army been dissolved?" Lee, "looking more the soldier than ever," one ragged veteran stated, grabbed a battle flag and raised it aloft. For the first time, Confederates saw their commanding general acting as a color-bearer. "His appearance raised a general tumult," Capt. John Esten Cooke stated. "The dilapidated figures started up from the ground, shouting and gesticulating with hands clenched above their heads."

With what Gen. William Mahone called "the retreating herd" brought under control, Lee relinquished the flag, turned his horse, Traveler, and slowly resumed his westward march.

"We Still Love You, General Lee"

Appomattox, Virginia, April 9, 1865

Virginia cavalryman Rawleigh Dunaway embodied the inner spirit of the Army of Northern Virginia when he wrote home in February 1865: "I have thought the matter over calmly & seriously & have made up my mind to follow that great & good man, Robt. E. Lee, wherever he may lead, to success or to ruin if it must be."

At Appomattox on Palm Sunday, it all ended. The Union army had surrounded what was left of Lee's forces. Grant proved as charitable in victory as he was unbending in war. There would be no revenge to poison the peace. "The Rebels are our countrymen again," Grant announced.

Lee left the meeting with Grant and rode back to his lines, erect as ever, eyes staring ahead. Confederates started to cheer, then broke ranks and crowded bareheaded around their beloved commander. "Men," Lee said, "we have fought the war together, and I have done the best I could for you. You will be paroled and go to your homes until exchanged." Tears swelled in his eyes. Lee could say no more than a choking "Goodbye."

As he rode away, an overcome soldier extended his arms and shouted: "I love you just as well as ever, General Lee!"

The next morning, with rain falling, Lee wrote his farewell address to his soldiers. He spoke the right words: "After four years of arduous service . . . unsurpassed courage and fortitude . . . steadfast to the last . . . duty faithfully performed." Lee concluded: "I earnestly pray that a merciful God will extend to you His blessing and protection." Staff officer Giles Cooke noticed that after completing the document, "the tears ran down the old hero's cheeks, and he gave way—for the first time that I ever knew him to do."

Throughout that day of defeat, Lee exhibited the same dignity and the same devotion to duty for which he was so revered.

Salute of Honor

Appomattox, Virginia, April 12, 1865

The final duty for the Army of Northern Virginia came on April 12, an overcast, chilly Wednesday. It was to surrender arms, cartridge boxes, and flags to the Union army. A long, silent column crossed the Appomattox River and made its way up to the village where the Union V Corps waited in line on both sides of the road.

Millett Thompson of the 13th New Hampshire remembered "how we . . . pitied and sympathized with these courageous Southern men who had fought for four long and dreary years all so stubbornly, so bravely and so well, and now, whipped, beaten, completely used up, were fully at our mercy—it was pitiable, sad, hard, and seemed to us altogether too bad."

Gen. Lawrence Chamberlain of Gettysburg fame was in charge of receiving the weapons and standards. He knew what the Confederates were experiencing. As the ragged Southerners approached the Union lines, a bugle rang out amid the shuffle of feet, and Federal soldiers shifted from order arms to carry arms— the marching salute. Startled Confederates found new life and immediately did the same. No cheer was given, no word spoken. Salute acknowledged salute. Honor answered honor.

REUNION AND REMEMBRANCES

T hat we are beaten is a self-evident fact," Gen. Bedford Forrest said in his last command to his cavalrymen. "Reason dictates and humanity demands that no more blood be shed. . . . You have been good soldiers, you can be good citizens. Obey the laws, preserve your honor, and the government to which you have surrendered can afford to be and will be magnanimous."

The senseless murder of Abraham Lincoln at war's end jeopardized that magnanimity. Moreover, reconciliation was going to require time. The war had exacted an enormous personal toll. Children lost their childhood; families lost loved ones; fathers, husbands, and brothers lost their lives. Burying the dead in no way buried the memories. Union and Confederate soldiers had fought one of the most destructive wars in history, and they had fought it with fierce passion. There were wounds that would be a long time healing, and scars no amount of time could remove.

As the postwar years ebbed, however, the great majority of Northern and Southern veterans aged gracefully. Each side came to understand and to appreciate what the other side had done. Johnny Rebs never apologized for what they had done, and Billy Yanks never asked them to do so.

That they had survived the four-year exposure to death produced a strange and strong comradeship. The 18th Mississippi's George Gibbs lost a leg in battle. In the twilight of his life, Gibbs mused: "I look back now, after so many years, on those turbulent times, and wonder where I found the fortitude, patience and endurance to pass through so many trying experiences." Rhode Islander Elisha Rhodes ended his war diary with the notation: "No more suffering. No more scenes of carnage and death. Thank God it is over . . . at last I am a simple citizen."

Sgt. Pitt Chambers, another Mississippi soldier, made a final observation about the war: "There are doubtless lessons in it for our good, as well as for the good of all the people of America, and I seem to realize more and more that God's hand is in it and that He has ordered it well."

Survivors of the long struggle gravitated together at parades, veterans' meeting, and especially at battlefield ceremonies. In October 1889, Maine's Joshua Lawrence Chamberlain spoke unforgettable lines at Gettysburg: "In great deeds something abides. On great fields something stays. Forms change and pass; bodies disappear; but spirits linger to consecrate ground for the vision-place of souls. . . . And reverent men and women from afar, and generations that know us not and that we know not of, heart-drawn to see where and by whom great things were suffered and done for them, shall come to this deathless field, to ponder and dream, and lo! The shadow of a mighty presence shall wrap them in its bosom, and the power of the vision pass into their souls."

Berry Benson was a South Carolina soldier who survived many battles as well as internment in a Northern prisoner-of-war camp. Only fifteen years after the guns ceased firing, Benson reflected on the past and the future: "Who knows but it may be given to us, after this life, to meet again in the old quarters . . . to hastily don our war gear while the monotonous patter of the long roll summons to battle? Who knows but again the old flags, ragged and torn, snapping in the wind, may face each other and flutter, pursuing and pursued, while the cries of victory fill a summer day? And after the battle, then the slain and wounded will arise, and all will meet together under the two flags, all sound and well, and there will be talking and laughter and cheers, and all will say: Did it not seem real? Was it not as in the old days?"

Thanks to those attitudes, and to those men, America still lives.

"In great deeds something abides. On great fields something stays. Forms change and pass; bodies disappear; but spirits linger to consecrate ground for the vision-place of souls. . . . and generations that know us not and that we know not of, heart-drawn to see where and by whom great things were suffered and done for them, shall come to this deathless field, to ponder and dream."

—Col. Joshua Lawrence Chamberlain

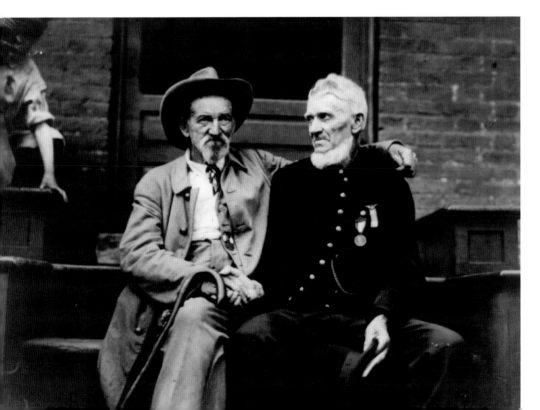

Opposite top: Confederate and Union veterans pose together for a photograph at the Gettysburg Reunion of 1913, which commemorated the fiftieth anniversary of the Battle of Gettysburg. Known as the Great Reunion, more than 50,000 veterans attended the ten-day event, from June 25 to July 4—the largest reunion of Civil War soldiers ever gathered. Courtesy Library of Congress Prints & Photographs Division, LC-DIG-ggbain-13841.

Left: Two veterans, gray and blue, shake hands at the 1913 Great Reunion. Courtesy Library of Congress Prints & Photographs Division, LC-USZ62-88416.

"I knew his goodness

of heart, his generosity . . . and above all his

desires to see all the people of the United

States enter again upon the full privileges of

citizenship and equality among all."

—Gen. Ulysses S. Grant

Lincoln Memorial

He looked and talked like his country: raw, rugged, and earnest. His concern for humanity, his never-failing belief in the people, made Abraham Lincoln among the most American of Americans. At the same time, he evolved into an astute political leader with the deft touch to mold and direct the nation through a horrible war.

Lincoln's apotheosis came at Ford's Theater. The assassin's bullet that killed him put a halo about his head. What followed was a paradox of history. The most unpopular man ever elected president became the most popular man of all the nation's greats. Years after the war, U. S. Grant wrote of Lincoln: "I knew his goodness of heart, his generosity, his yielding disposition, his desire to have everybody happy, and above all his desires to see all the people of the United States enter again upon the full privileges of citizenship and equality among all."

Today, in a Washington monument that has with time become a temple, Abraham Lincoln broods over the nation he gave his life to preserve.

The Lincoln Memorial dedication ceremony, Washington, D.C., May 30, 1922.
Courtesy Library of Congress Prints & Photographs Division, LC-USZ62-58706.

The Final Visit

Gen. Robert E. Lee, Stonewall Jackson Gravesite, Lexington, Virginia *(opposite)*

In late summer of 1865, Lee accepted the presidency of bankrupt Washington College in Lexington, Virginia (today called Washington and Lee University). "I have led the young men of the South in battle," Lee explained. "I have seen many of them fall under my standard. I shall devote my remaining energies to training young men to do their duty in life."

Lee spent his last five years in making the little college one of the finest liberal arts schools in America. At his death in 1870, a whole nation mourned.

The Lexington years were not especially happy for the aging general. "Traveler is my only companion," Lee told a friend. "I may also say my pleasure. He and I, whenever practicable, wander out in the mountains and enjoy sweet confidence." Their route often took them by the grave of Lee's greatest lieutenant, Stonewall Jackson. Lee would stand there silently. Nothing needed to be said. The two commanders had always communicated almost without speaking.

Fittingly, they are now buried within walking distance of each other.

"I have led the young men of the South in battle. I have seen many of them fall under my standard.

I shall devote my remaining energies to training young men to do their duty in life."

—Gen. Robert E. Lee

The Jackson gravesite today, in a photograph taken by Mort Künstler.

"...Swords into Plowshares"

For many Confederates, anticipated joy at going home changed abruptly on arrival to heartache. Josiah Reams returned to McNairy County, Tennessee, to find his family decimated. "My father and stepmother [had] died. My only brother was killed ...and a half brother on the Union side ... died. So our home was broken up and I was penniless."

Such was part of the cost of keeping intact the nation Lincoln considered "the last great hope of earth." After Theodore Upson received his discharge from Sherman's army and joined his wife on their Indiana farm, he wrote: "From those who have lived to return comes no words of regrets. They are content their duty is done, and well done. What matters the loss of all these years! What matters the trials, the sickness, the wounds! What we went out to do is done. The war is ended, and the Union is saved!"

"From **those who have lived to return** comes no words of regrets. They are **content their duty is done,** and well done. What matters the loss of all these years! What matters the trials, the sickness, the wounds! What we went out to do is done. **The war is ended, and the Union is saved!**"

—Pvt. Theodore Upson, 100th Indiana

SELECTED PORTRAITS

LEADERS OF THE UNION

Abraham Lincoln
(1809–65), President

Ulysses S. Grant
(1822–85), General in chief of the U.S. Army

William Tecumseh Sherman
(1820–91), General

Leaders of the Confederacy

Jefferson Davis

(1808–89), President

Robert E. Lee

(1807–70), General in chief

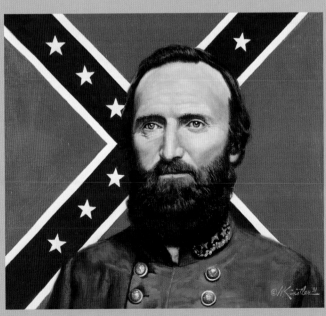

Thomas "Stonewall" Jackson

(1824–63), Lieutenant General

THE UNION

John Buford
(1826–63), Illinois

Joshua Lawrence Chamberlain
(1828–1914), Maine

David Glasgow Farragut
(1801–70), U.S. Navy

Winfield Scott Hancock
(1824–86), Pennsylvania (detail)

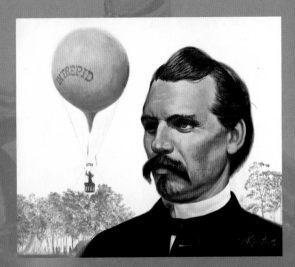

Thaddeus S. C. Lowe
(1832–1913), Union Army Balloon Corps

George Gordon Meade
(1815–72), Army of the Potamac

George B. McClellan
(1826–85), Army of the Potamac

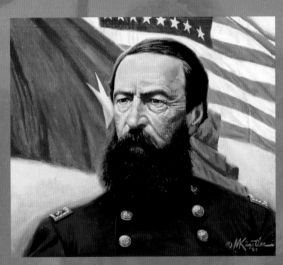

David Porter
(1813–91), U.S. Navy

John F. Reynolds
(1820–63), Major General, Pennsylvania (detail)

Philip Sheridan
(1831–88), Ohio (detail)

THE CONFEDERACY

William Barksdale
(1821–63), Mississippi

P. G. T. Beauregard,
(1818–93), Louisiana

Nathan Bedford Forrest
(1821–77), Tennessee

John Brown Gordon
(1832–1904), Georgia

Ambrose Powell Hill

(1825–65), Virginia

John Bell Hood

(1831–79), Texas

James Longstreet

(1821–1904), South Carolina

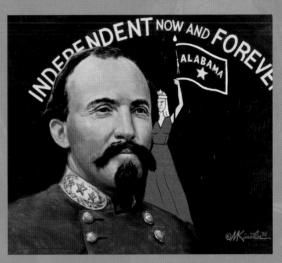

John Hunt Morgan

(1825–64), Alabama

J. E. B. Stuart

(1833–64), Virginia

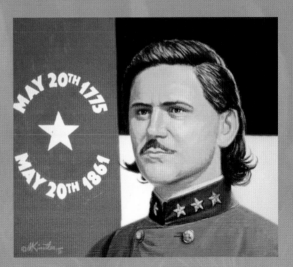

Zebulon B. Vance

(1830–94), North Carolina

BIBLIOGRAPHY

Annals of the War Written by Leading Participants North and South. Philadelphia: Times Publishing, 1879.

Bennett, Brian A. *Sons of Old Monroe: A Regimental History of Patrick O'Rorke's 140th New York Volunteer Infantry.* Dayton, OH: Morningside House, 1992.

Benson, Berry. *Berry Benson's Civil War Book: Memoirs of a Confederate Scout and Sharpshooter.* Athens: University of Georgia Press, 1962.

Berkeley, Henry Robinson. *Four Years in the Confederate Artillery.* Chapel Hill: University of North Carolina Press, 1961.

Bilby, Joseph G. *Remember Fontenoy! The 69th New York and the Irish Brigade in the Civil War.* Highstown, NJ: Longstreet House, 1995.

Blackford, Susan Leigh, comp. *Letters from Lee's Army.* New York: Charles Scribner's Sons, 1947.

Blackford, William W. *War Years with Jeb Stuart.* New York: Charles Scribner's Sons, 1945.

Borcke, Heros von. *Memoirs of the Confederate War for Independence.* 2 vols. Edinburgh: W. Blackwood & Sons, 1866.

Bragg, Julius N. *Letters of a Confederate Surgeon, 1861–1865.* Camden, AR: privately printed, 1960.

Brown, Dee Alexander. *Grierson's Raid.* Dayton, OH: Morningside Bookshop, 1981.

Buck, Lucy R. *Sad Earth, Sweet Heaven: The Diary of Lucy Rebecca Buck during the War between the States.* Birmingham, AL: Buck Publishing, 1992.

Buell, Augustus C. *The Cannoneer: Recollections of Service in the Army of the Potomac.* Washington, DC: National Tribune, 1890.

[Caffey, Thomas E.] *Battle-fields of the South: From Bull Run to Fredericksburg.* 2 vols. London: Smith, Elder & Co., 1864.

Caldwell, James F. J. *The History of a Brigade of South Carolinians First Known as "Gregg's" and Subsequently as "McCowan's" Brigade.* Philadelphia: King & Baird, 1866.

Calkins, William W. *The History of the One Hundred and Fourth Regiment of Illinois Volunteer Infantry, War of the Great Rebellion, 1862–1865.* Chicago: Donohue & Henneberry, 1895.

Catton, Bruce. *Glory Road.* Garden City, NY: Doubleday, 1952.

——. *Mr. Lincoln's Army.* Garden City, NY: Doubleday, 1951.

——. *A Stillness at Appomattox.* Garden City, NY: Doubleday, 1953.

Chamberlain, Joshua Lawrence. *"Bayonet! Forward": My Civil War Reminiscences.* Gettysburg, PA: Stan Clark Military Books, 1994.

Chamberlayne, John Hampden. *Ham Chamberlayne—Virginian: Letters and Papers of an Artillery Officer in the War for Southern Independence, 1861–1865.* Richmond, VA: Dietz, 1932.

Chambers, William Pitt. *Blood & Sacrifice: The Civil War Journal of a Confederate Soldier.* Huntington, WV: Blue Acorn Press, 1994.

Conyngham, David P. *The Irish Brigade and Its Campaigns.* Glasgow: R. & T. Washbourne, 1866.

Cook, Joel. *The Siege of Richmond.* Philadelphia: G. W. Childs, 1862.

Corson, William C. *My Dear Jennie.* Richmond, VA: Dietz Press, 1982.

Crews, Edward W., and Timothy A. Parrish. *14th Virginia Infantry.* Lynchburg, VA: H. E. Howard, 1995.

Current, Richard N., et al., eds. *Encyclopedia of the Confederacy.* 4 vols. New York: Simon & Schuster, 1993.

Davis, Archie K. *Boy Colonel of the Confederacy: The Life and Times of Henry King Burgwyn.* Chapel Hill: University of North Carolina Press, 1985.

Davis, William C. *Brother Against Brother: The Civil War Begins.* Alexandria, VA: Time-Life Books, 1983.

——. *First Blood: Fort Sumter to Bull Run.* Alexandria, VA: Time-Life Books, 1983.

——. *Jefferson Davis: The Man and His Hour.* New York: HarperCollins, 1991.

Dickert, D. Augustus. *History of Kershaw's Brigade.* Newberry, SC: E. H. Aull, 1899.

Donaldson, Francis A. *Inside the Army of the Potomac: The Civil War Experiences of Francis A. Donaldson.* Mechanicsburg, PA: Stackpole Books, 1998.

Dooley, John E. *John Dooley, Confederate Soldier: His War Journal.* Washington, DC: Georgetown University Press, 1945.

Driver, Robert J., Jr. *The 1st and 2nd Rockbridge Artillery.* Lynchburg, VA: H. E. Howard, 1987.

——. *1st Virginia Cavalry.* Lynchburg, VA: H. E. Howard, 1991.

Duncan, Richard R. *Beleaguered Winchester: A Virginia Community at War, 1861–1865.* Baton Rouge: Louisiana State University Press, 2007.

Duncan, Russell. *Where Death and Glory Meet: Colonel Robert Gould Shaw and the 54th Massachusetts Infantry.* Athens: University of Georgia Press, 1999.

Edmondson, James K. *My Dear Emma: War Letters of Col. James K. Edmondson, 1861–1865.* Verona, VA: McClure Printing, 1978.

Edmondston, Catherine D. *Journal of a Secesh Lady: The Diary of Catherine Ann Devereux Edmondston, 1860–1866.* Raleigh: North Carolina Department of Archives and History, 1979.

Fisk, Wilbur. *Hard Marching Every Day: The Civil War Letters of Private Wilbur Fisk.* Lawrence: University Press of Kansas, 1992.

Freeman, Douglas Southall. *Lee's Lieutenants: A Study in Command.* 3 vols. New York: Charles Scribner's Sons, 1942–44.

——. *R. E. Lee: A Biography.* 4 vols. New York: Charles Scribner's Sons, 1934–35.

Fremantle, James A. L. *Three Months in the Southern States, April–June, 1863.* Edinburgh: William Blackwood & Sons, 1863.

Gerrish, Theodore. *Army Life: A Private's Reminiscences of the Civil War.* Portland, ME: Hoyt, Fogg & Donham, 1882.

Glatthaar, Joseph T. *General's Lee's Army.* New York: Free Press, 2008.

Gleeson, Ed. *Rebel Sons of Erin: A Civil War Unit History of the Tenth Tennessee Infantry Regiment Irish, Confederate States Volunteers.* Indianapolis: Guild Press of Indiana, 1993.

Gordon, John B. *Reminiscences of the Civil War.* New York: Charles Scribner's Sons, 1903.

Goree, Thomas J. *Longstreet's Aide: The Civil War Letters of Major Thomas J. Goree.* Charlottesville: University Press of Virginia, 1995.

Gragg, Rod. *Confederate Goliath: The Battle of Fort Fisher.* New York: HarperCollins, 1991.

———. *Covered with Glory: The 26th North Carolina Infantry at Gettysburg.* New York: HarperCollins, 2000.

Graham, James A. *The James A. Graham Papers, 1861–1864.* Chapel Hill: University of North Carolina Press, 1928.

Grant, Ulysses S. *Personal Memoirs of U. S. Grant.* 2 vols. New York: C. L. Webster, 1885–86.

Gregory, G. Howard. *38th Virginia Infantry.* Lynchburg, VA: H. E. Howard, 1988.

Gunn, Ralph White. *24th Virginia Infantry.* Lynchburg, VA: H. E. Howard, 1987.

Heidler, David S., and Jeanne T. Heidler, eds. *Encyclopedia of the American Civil War.* 5 vols. Santa Barbara, CA: ABC-CLIO, 2000.

Hennessy, John J. *Return to Bull Run.* New York: Simon & Schuster, 1993.

Henry, Robert Selph, ed. *As They Saw Forrest: Some Recollections and Comments of Contemporaries.* Jackson, TN: McCowat-Mercer Press, 1956.

Holmes, Emma. *The Diary of Miss Emma Holmes, 1861–1866.* Baton Rouge: Louisiana State University Press, 1979.

Hunter, Alexander. *Johnny Reb and Billy Yank.* New York: Neale Publishing, 1903.

Jackson, Mary Anna. *Memoirs of Stonewall Jackson, By His Widow.* Louisville, KY: Prentice Press, 1895.

Jones, J. B. *A Rebel War Clerk's Diary at the Confederate States Capital.* 2 vols. Philadelphia: J. B. Lippincott, 1866.

Jones, J. William. *Personal Reminiscences, Anecdotes, and Letters of Gen. Robert E. Lee.* New York: D. Appleton, 1875.

Jones, Terry L. *Lee's Tigers: The Louisiana Infantry in the Army of Northern Virginia.* Baton Rouge: Louisiana State University Press, 1987.

Judson, Amos M. *History of the Eighty-third Regiment Pennsylvania Volunteers.* Erie, PA: B. F. H. Lynn, 1865.

Lanier, Richard. *The Angel of Marye's Heights.* Fredericksburg, VA: Fredericksburg Press, 1961.

Lyman, Theodore. *Meade's Headquarters, 1863–1865: Letters of Colonel Theodore Lyman from the Wilderness to Appomattox.* Boston: Atlantic Monthly Press, 1922.

McDonald, Cornelia. *A Diary with Reminiscences of the War and Refugee Life in the Shenandoah Valley, 1860–1865.* Nashville: Cullum & Ghertner, 1934.

McGavock, Randal W. *Pen and Sword: The Life and Journals of Randal W. McGavock.* Nashville: Tennessee Historical Commission, 1959.

McGuire, Judith B. *Diary of a Southern Refugee during the War.* New York: E. J. Hale & Sons, 1867.

McPherson, James M. *Battle Cry of Freedom.* New York: Oxford University Press, 1988.

Mahon, Michael G., ed. *Winchester Divided: The Civil War Diaries of Julia Chase and Laura Lee.* Mechanicsburg, PA: Stackpole Books, 2002.

Marshall, Charles. *An Aide-de-Camp of Lee.* Boston: Little, Brown, 1927.

Mosby, John S. *Mosby's War Reminiscences and Stuart's Cavalry Campaigns.* Boston: George A. Jones, 1887.

Nash, Eugene A. *A History of the Forty-fourth Regiment, New York Volunteer Infantry, in the Civil War, 1861–1865.* Chicago: R. R. Donnelley & Sons, 1911.

Oates, Stephen B. *With Malice toward None: The Life of Abraham Lincoln.* New York: Harper & Row, 1977.

———. *A Woman of Valor: Clara Barton and the Civil War.* New York: Free Press, 1994.

Oates, William C. *The War between the Union and the Confederacy and Its Lost Opportunities, with a History of the 15th Alabama Regiment and the Forty-eight Battles in Which It Was Engaged.* New York: Neale, 1905.

O'Reilly, Francis Augustin. *The Fredericksburg Campaign.* Baton Rouge: Louisiana State University Press, 2003.

Pender, William Dorsey. *The General to His Lady: The Civil War Letters of William Dorsey Pender to Fanny Pender.* Chapel Hill: University of North Carolina Press, 1965.

Piston, William Garrett. *Wilson's Creek: The Second Battle of the Civil War and The Men Who Fought It.* Chapel Hill: University of North Carolina Press, 2000.

Pullen, John J. *The Twentieth Maine.* Philadelphia: J. B. Lippincott, 1957.

Ramage, James A. *Rebel Raider: The Life of General John Hunt Morgan.* Lexington: University of Kentucky Press, 1986.

Rhodes, Elisha H. *All for the Union: A History of the 2nd Rhode Island Infantry in the Great War of the Rebellion.* Lincoln, RI: Andrew Mowbray, 1985.

Riggs, Susan A. *21st Virginia Infantry.* Lynchburg, VA: H. E. Howard, 1991.

Ripley, Eliza McHatton. *From Flag to Flag.* New York: D. Appleton, 1889.

Robertson, James I., Jr. *18th Virginia Infantry.* Lynchburg, VA: H. E. Howard, 1984.

———. *General A. P. Hill: The Story of a Confederate Warrior.* New York: Random House, 1987.

———. *Soldiers Blue and Gray.* Columbia: University of South Carolina Press, 1988.

———. *Stonewall Jackson: The Man, The Soldier, The Legend.* New York: Macmillan, 1997.

Scheibert, Justus. *Seven Months in the Rebel States during the North American War, 1863.* Tuscaloosa, AL: Confederate Publishing Co., 1958.

Schurz, Carl. *The Reminiscences of Carl Schurz.* 3 vols. New York: McClure, 1907–08.

Sears, Stephen W. *Chancellorsville.* Boston: Houghton Mifflin, 1996.

———. *Landscape Turned Red: The Battle of Antietam.* New Haven, CT: Ticknor & Fields, 1983.

———. *To the Gates of Richmond: The Peninsula Campaign.* New York: Ticknor & Fields, 1992.

Sherman, William T. *Memoirs of General William T. Sherman.* 2 vols. New York: D. Appleton, 1875.

Smith, Thomas W. *"We Have It Damn Hard Out Here": The Civil War Letters of Sergeant Thomas W. Smith, 6th Pennsylvania Cavalry.* Kent, OH: Kent State University Press, 1999.

Sorrel, G. Moxley. *Recollections of a Confederate Staff Officer.* New York: Neale, 1905.

Southern Historical Society Papers. 52 vols. Richmond: Southern Historical Society, 1876–1952.

Stiles, Kenneth. *4th Virginia Cavalry.* Lynchburg, VA: H. E. Howard, 1985.

Stiles, Robert. *Four Years under Marse Robert.* New York: Neale, 1903.

Stilwell, William R., and Robert Mosley, ed. *The Stilwell Letters: A Georgian in Longtreet's Corps, Army of Northern Virginia.* Macon, GA: Mercer University Press, 2002.

Strong, George Templeton. *Diary of the Civil War, 1860–1865.* New York: Macmillan, 1962.

Taylor, Walter H. *General Lee: His Campaigns in Virginia, 1861–1865, with Personal Reminiscences.* Norfolk, VA: Nusbaum Book and Art Co., 1906.

Thomas, Emory M. *Bold Dragoon: The Life of J. E. B. Stuart.* New York: Harper & Row, 1986.

———. *Robert E. Lee: A Biography.* New York: W. W. Norton, 1995.

Thompson, S. Millett. *Thirteenth Regiment of New Hampshire Volunteer Infantry in the War of the Rebellion, 1861–1865.* Boston: Houghton Mifflin, 1888.

Todd, William. *The Seventy-ninth Highlanders, New York Volunteers, in the War of the Rebellion, 1861–1865.* Albany: Brandon & Barton, 1886.

Trueheart, Charles W. *Rebel Brothers: The Civil War Letters of the Truehearts.* College Station: Texas A&M University Press, 1995.

Tunnard, William H. *A Southern Record: The History of the Third Louisiana Infantry.* Baton Rouge: printed for the author, 1866.

U. S. War Dept., comp. *War of the Rebellion: A Compilation of the Official Records of the Union and Confederate Armies.* 128 vols. Washington, DC: Government Printing Office, 1880–1902.

Upson, Theodore F. *With Sherman to the Sea: The Civil War Letters, Diaries & Reminiscences of Theodore F. Upson.* Baton Rouge: Louisiana State University Press, 1943.

Welsh, Peter. *Irish Green and Union Blue: The Civil War Letters of Peter Welsh, Color Sergeant, 28th Regiment Massachusetts Volunteers.* New York: Fordham University Press, 1986.

Whitman, Walt. *Memoranda during the War.* Bloomington: Indiana University Press, 1962.

Wiley, Bell Irvin. *The Life of Billy Yank.* Indianapolis: Bobbs-Merrill, 1952.

———. *The Life of Johnny Reb.* Indianapolis: Bobbs-Merrill, 1943.

Williamson, James J. *Mosby's Rangers: A Record of the Operations of the Forty-third Virginia Cavalry from Its Organization to the Surrender.* New York: R. B. Kenyon, 1896.

Wills, Brian Steel. *A Battle from the Start: The Life of Nathan Bedford Forrest.* New York: HarperCollins, 1992.

Wise, John S. *The End of an Era.* Boston: Houghton Mifflin, 1902.

Wolseley, Garnet J. M. "General Forrest." *United Service Magazine,* 127, April–May 1892.

Young, William A., and Patricia C. Young. *56th Virginia Infantry.* Lynchburg, VA: H. E. Howard, 1990.

INDEX OF PAINTINGS

All measurements in inches

INDEX